APPROACHING THE
DECADE
OF
SHOCK!

APPROACHING THE
DECADE
OF
SHOCK

By

Clifford Wilson, Ph.D.

and

John Weldon

Foreword by Tim LaHaye

MASTER BOOKS

A Division of CLP

San Diego, California

APPROACHING THE DECADE OF SHOCK

Copyright © 1978
MASTER BOOKS, A Division of CLP
P. O. Box 15666
San Diego, California 92115

Library of Congress Catalog Card Number 78-52320
ISBN 0-89051-044-X

Cataloging in Publication Data
Wilson, Clifford A. 1923-
   Approaching the decade of shock.
   1. Ecology. 2. World Politics. 3. Eschatology. 4. Bible— prophecies. I. Weldon, John 1948-   , jt. auth. II. Title. III. Title: Decade of shock.
                                236   78-52320

Printed in the United States of America

Cover by Marvin Ross

Foreword

Civilization is on a collision course with destiny, and the pace is increasing at a frightening rate of speed. Catastrophic events during this "Decade of Depression" (the 70's) are increasing in such size and intensity that one gets the dreaded feeling something momentous is about to occur. I sometimes liken the rapidly increasing pace of life to a runaway train going downhill with the engine jammed wide open. It is only a matter of time before our accepted form of civilization is derailed completely.

Although I thought I was generally aware of what is happening on this place we call planet earth, not until I read *Decade of Shock* did I realize how close to the end things really are. Dr. Wilson and John Weldon are to be commended for the interesting way they have woven together the latest facts of science to show that the world is on the verge of its greatest shock since the days of Noah.

The thing that intrigued me was that they did not rest their case on the political, economic, and spiritual signs with which we are all familiar, but included key trends in such vital areas as ecology, pollution, and science. Their research convincingly demonstrates that we are rapidly approaching the time when the only solution to the world's problems is a one world dictator—just as the Bible predicts.

I found this book interesting, compelling, and an extremely valuable library of resource material that every person should read—especially teachers and students of the Bible.

Tim LaHaye, Chancellor
Christian Heritage College

Contents

Chapter 1

Watch The Calendar— Then The Clock

We can't stop the world's revolution, and so the years rush by. We can't even stop its rotation—so we must face the realities of daily situations. The days come and go . . . and merge into weeks . . . into months . . . . . into years. . . . *and the years merge into decades.*

This writing begins in 1978—less than two years from the commencement of *The Decade of Shock*. We can't stop the clock. We can't command the sun to stand still. We can't go back to the horse and buggy days when the steam train was a dream and rockets to the moon were laughable science fiction.

Nor can we hide in a zoo with the ostriches and bury our heads under the sand. There is no more sand under which to bury. The Arabs bought it all with their petro-dollars, and alas! there is no place to hide. Already we are made vividly aware of the impending birth pains of The Decade of Shock.

We are faced with two alternatives, unless we have already chosen self-annihilation—and we have chosen the latter by *default* if we are refusing to face the facts. The sun will rise, the earth will rotate, and soon it will have revolved—once, then twice . . . and we are in that decade. Refusing to see the sun rise in the morning won't stop its rising . . . and won't keep us from *1980*.

TWO OPTIONS

Presuming we *will* face the facts, what are the two alternatives? Put bluntly, they are to be hellishly materialistic or to be totally committed to spiritual truth. The former might deny or ignore the latter, but the latter can realistically recognize the facts of life and endorse the need for dramatic preparations of a deadly nature.

We thought the preparations for World War II were frightening, and they were. As a result of that catastrophe we now know a new dimension of terror—and not only because of Hiroshima and Nagasaki. Human beings in gas ovens . . . human skin for lamp-shades . . . children machine-gunned in their already-prepared mass graves . . . and a great deal more inhumanity that is best not described.

The situations we now face again embrace all those possibilities and ever so much more. Hitler's name has given over to others such as Idi Amin, and gas ovens were replaced by flaming human torches in some of the Vietnam incidents. There is no Hiroshima yet, but we are merely playing a waiting game—waiting until one side has built up a big enough stockpile, with new terror weapons, so that the other side will be blackmailed into submission. And it may not be atomic blackmail, as we shall see.

A SERIES OF INTERACTING CRISES

The consequences and threats facing us are not only in the realms of nuclear weapons and atomic warfare. The next decade will bring us to a whole series of interacting crises, each of them far-reaching in their potential consequences.

This is a situation different than any the world has ever faced before. Consistently, through the centuries, only *one* major crisis at a time has been sufficient to bring nations into open conflict and war. Never before have the issues been so widespread as now, with not just one crisis facing us, but a large number of interlocking areas, any one of which would have been sufficient in a previous generation to hurl the world into war. The devastating nature of atomic warfare is the great deterrent to international suicide, but interlocking crises face us in the realms of energy, oil, famines, economics, differing ideologies, political changes, national and international aspirations, the emergence of Third World countries, and Middle East tensions of various types . . . and these are only some of the major areas that are interrelated, yet separate.

That dread little button has not yet been pressed in the "space age seventies," but there certainly is no guarantee that it will not be pressed in the alarming eighties . . . for the eighties will be the *Decade of Shock*.

In this book we consider some of the basic facts and issues, and our method is to analyze writings by experts in their various fields. The results are not always pleasant reading, but they are an honest appraisal.

Perhaps such an appraisal can have some small part in molding opinion. At least it can inform us of the stark realities by which we are surrounded, and possibly it can help us toward making mature judgments as to our own attitudes, reactions, and even responsibilities. We hope so. Despite a difficult future, we must all be as responsible as we can, within our own sphere of influence.

The fact is, we ourselves come up with some conclusions that are different from those we would like to find. For instance, contrary to public opinion, current U.S. policy does not rule out the possibility of using nuclear weapons. There is a very real possibility of fighting *limited* nuclear wars. This applies especially with regard to a number of potential trouble spots around the world.

We Westerners tend to think that nuclear weapons will not be used because it would be "national suicide" to do so. That might well be true, but decisions at even the highest levels are made by individuals. Those individuals

would be just as dead if shot by a bullet as with a retalia-
tory atomic weapon. They could even be blackmailed or
otherwise forced into an action with disastrous consequences, in order to save their own lives.

THAT MIDDLE EAST TIME BOMB

It is openly claimed that Israel has atomic weapons. It
is also widely recognized that Israel, of all nations, is
unlikely to submit to blackmail of any kind. Munich and
Entebbe alike, as well as reprisal sorties and more into
Lebanon, have made it clear that Israel will fight to the
bitter end and never surrender. What if, in one of these
encounters, the successes of 1948, 1967, and 1974 are not
repeated? 1974 was not as swiftly decisive as 1967, and
even a few extra days of modern "conventional" warfare
would add enormously to the costs. What then if the
number of days were to be lengthened a little, into just a
few weeks? We no longer think of wars lasting several
years as they did with World Wars I and II.

We are all—always—only days away from the possibility
of sudden takeover. What does Israel (or another nation in
desperate straits) do if they are surrounded by implacable
enemies? Do they say to themselves, "Well, we have
atomic bombs but we can't use those of course. That
wouldn't be fair play. It might even cause New York to be
bombed. After all, we only built our atomic arsenal as a
deterrent. We'll just have to surrender to those nice Arabs
now."

No way. And we know it! The Middle East is a time
bomb, its explosion point pushed back almost monthly.
Those tick-tick-tick sounds are ominously loud. The explosion might even come before the Decade of Shock—the
1980's. Maybe we're optimistic. At any time we could
find ourselves plunged into that war that we fear will end
it all.

A FINGER ON THE BUTTON

There have been no less than eight occasions since 1953
when at least the limited use of nuclear bombs was serious-

ly considered by the United States.[1] The best-known was the Cuban missile crisis of 1962, but it was not the only one. Others included its threatened use against North Korea during the Korean War, again during the Laotian crisis of 1961, later still in Vietnam, also against the Chinese mainland, and even in Europe during a Berlin crisis. We currently have nuclear weapons in South Korea, and we have threatened to use them.[2] What other occasions besides those we have listed have there been—but are known only to a handful of leaders?

Nor is that all. We tend to think that it depends only on "us." America is a highly responsible nation, but yet has come to the brink of nuclear war. "That" button has nearly been pressed.

But what about Russia? Have they (like the United States) come to the brink eight + times since 1953?

And what about countries of the Third World? If an American college boy can (on paper) construct an atomic bomb, and if Israel has them, do we seriously think that their manufacture and use will be forever restricted to the major powers? If we *do* think that, we are burying our heads in that nonexistent sand again.

We have said that many people today think that nuclear war is out of the question because it could lead to the total destruction of the human race. Unfortunately our leaders and the opposing leaders do not necessarily agree. In our next chapter we consider some sobering facts and opinions from men who should know.

Footnotes: Chapter 1

1. Sidney Lens, "The Arms Race: A Primer," *The Progressive,* October, 1977, p. 41.
2. W.R. VanCleave, S.T. Cohen, "Nuclear Aspects of Future U.S. Security Policy in Asia," *Orbis,* Fall, 1975. p. 1152 ff.

Chapter 2

Nuclear War?

Even a first use of nuclear weapons by the United States is not ruled out. Former Defense Secretary Donald Rumsfeld warns, "We do not preclude even a first use of nuclear weapons in the defense of our interests."[1] The problem is that a limited nuclear war would, almost of necessity, escalate into full nuclear war. Robert McNamara has stated, "Once you use them (small nuclear weapons) you use everything else; you can't keep them limited, you'll destroy everything." The nuclear warhead is so destructive, it can be countered only by a more destructive warhead, which demands escalation, particularly when each side knows the other side can within minutes launch bombs that will destroy them.[2]

Bernard T. Feld states: "Not only has there been no convincing demonstration of the feasibility of limited use of nuclear bombs as a means of controlling a conventional conflict, but the thesis that any such use must inevitably escalate into a full-scale war remains unrefuted."[3]

It is this advocacy of the limited use of nuclear weapons that is one factor increasing the chances of world war. On the other hand, if we don't threaten their use—*and mean it*—our enemies will take advantage of our soft position. This is simply a fact of history. *There are no easy answers.*

A further concern recently expressed by White House spokesman Jody Powell was the increased chances of starting war via high energy chemical laser killer satellites in orbit. *The Los Angeles Times* of November 8, 1977, quoted Powell as stating:

> The deployment of killer satellites by The United States and the Soviet Union would increase the chances of an anti-satellite "first strike" in space . . . . We are concerned about the prospect of the major powers becoming involved in an accelerated arms race in this area.

In another article *The Washington Post* quoted an arms control authority: "There are so many military satellites in space and so many Buck Rogers methods of knocking them out today that the [1967 space] treaty is a joke."[4]

Recently Russia has conducted several tests of its "hunter-killer" satellites, and the Department of Defense has announced that it is aggressively pursuing defensive measures to protect U.S. satellites.[5] One article in *The Inter-Dependent,* a publication of the United Nations Association of the United States, also pointed out that the Pentagon is "interested in the possibility of using nuclear bombs or chemicals to create a hole in the earth's ozone layer above enemy countries, thus exposing them to intense ultraviolet radiation."[5a]

Ponder *that* frightening possibility—nature itself turned into an instrument of war! These days it is seriously suggested by some authorities that perhaps the earth's atmosphere underwent great changes at the time of the Biblical flood: that a protective water-vapor canopy collapsed, leading to increased radiations of various kinds, and maybe dramatically shortening the human life span. Now we moderns talk in all seriousness about dramatically localizing radiation effects, with devastating effects on all who happen to live in that region.

WHAT ARE THE ODDS—"BEFORE 1984?"

Many authorities openly declare their belief that the world will experience a nuclear war. In addition to current stockpiles, both the U.S. and Russia manufacture 2,200 hydrogen bombs per year—a staggering 6 per day.[6] In 1976 the nonnuclear-weapon countries had the capacity to make over 500 nuclear bombs per year.[7] Nobel Laureate Alfred Kastler stated in late 1977, "There is no need to be a great scholar or great prophet to see that the human race is rushing toward its suicide."[8]

Although to most people the idea of nuclear war is "unthinkable"—and about as probable as an invasion from Mars—a good number of both military planners and arms limitation experts believe it will happen. Bernard T. Feld has put the position well when he reminded us that the world is entering upon perilous times and indeed that it is possibly the most dangerous period in the entire history of the world. He made the point that in his judgment the odds were about 1 in 3 that a nuclear weapon would be used in a situation of conflict before the year 1984, and he went on to suggest that the chances were greater than 50/50 for nuclear war to take place in the remaining years of this century. In his judgment, the events of past history would hardly justify a conclusion that was any less pessimistic.[9]

BEFORE 2000 A.D.—
WITHOUT "ACTS OF MADNESS"

Another relevant comment is that from Carl Friedrich von Weizsacker, Director of the *Institute of Man* of the Max Planch Society in Starnberg and recipient of the Frankfurt Peace Prize. He gave as his judgment that continuing technical progress in the current world in which we live with its political set-up, means that it is highly probable that there will be an atomic war to engulf the world before the end of this century. He went on to suggest that such a statement did not mean that it was necessary to assume that acts of madness would occur. He put out his view that all that was necessary for his belief to come

to fulfillment was for governments of the world to continue to act as they do now.[10]

He notes the chance that one country may develop a
significant arms lead over the other, or a situation may
develop (there are many possible ways) in which the first
side to strike will win. "According to the classical rules of
power politics, in such a situation war will break out
sooner or later."[11]

William Epstein, Special Consultant on Disarmament to
the UN, has worked on arms control problems for a quarter century. In his book, *The Last Chance: Nuclear Proliferation and Arms Control,* he sees the possibility of a
nuclear holocaust as having risen to a near certainty.[12]

In September, 1977, more than 200 experts from 25
countries met in Paris for the annual conference of the
International Institute for Strategic Studies. They included
government officials, technical experts, senior military
officers, intelligence officers, professional diplomats, etc.
Their conclusions were at best gloomy. The danger of war
was seen as almost inevitable; in the words of one correspondent, "An extremely gloomy picture can be painted
showing that there appears little that anyone or anything
can do to stop an apparently inevitable march toward
more conflict . . . . "[13]

The battle lines appear to be drawn more between the
North-South nations than between the East-West ones—
that is, the division is between the have and the have-not
nations. The United Nations was viewed as obsolete in
terms of offering any real solutions. In the near future,
when Third World nations are faced with mass starvation,
will they sit down and die? Nobel Laureate and Emeritus
Professor of Physics at the University of Paris, Alfred
Kastler, thinks not. It is his view that U.S. troops will
never again be involved in a "conventional" Vietnam-type
war in any other Asian country. He suggests that, if treaties
mean anything, nuclear war is more than a possibility. He
argues that nations will not be prepared to die without
protest, and that there will be a revolt. Even if people do
not have enough food to eat they will have enough weap-

ons because billions of dollars are being spent every year on armaments. Soon it is probable that one billion well-fed people will be confronted by four billion who are starving—and the billion well-fed people will have 10,000 hydrogen bombs available, ready to be used, possibly in a time of panic. Kastler makes the point that the dreadful scenario which could ensue has a 99 percent chance of actually occurring unless governments undergo radical changes of attitudes.[14]

U.S. CAN ONLY DEFEND ASIAN COUNTRIES WITH NUCLEAR WEAPONS

Significantly, the above conference concluded that the probability of war was especially acute in the Third World countries, many of which may soon have nuclear weapons themselves. Other studies show that the military situation in Asia is precarious at best, and that the U.S., for a variety of reasons, can defend free countries in Asia only via the use of nuclear weapons.[15]

Finally, here are the considerations of five experts of a Harvard-M.I.T. Arms Control Seminar, held in late 1975.[16] Their basic conclusions were as follows:

1. Nuclear war in some form is likely before the end of the century.
2. It will probably result directly from proliferation.
3. If nations are to survive, they may have to surrender their sovereignty.
4. The public is too complacent about the prospects of nuclear war.

NUCLEAR WAR: THE DANGER OF COMPLACENCY

Arms Strategist and Political Economy Professor, Thomas Schelling, of Harvard has stated:

> We seem to be experiencing an almost inevitable drift toward less world order . . . . we have now a period of relative public confidence that nu-

clear war is not imminent. This complacency can itself be a danger.

Given Rathjen's estimate of at least a thousand reactors producing enough material for 50,000 bombs by the end of the century, what is now being done or what can be done to prevent the nuclear weapons industry from getting out of control? I think that nothing is being done—or even being contemplated—to cope with the problem.

Harvard Professor, George Kistiakowsky, states:

I estimate that the probability of a nuclear war occurring in any 12-month period ahead is actually increasing.

There are no cases in history of absolutely insane arms races ending peacefully. Arms races usually end up in wars.

Unless something totally unpredictable or unforeseeable happens . . . . The chance of a nuclear war is quite substantial.

Former Department of Defense specialist and current M.I.T. Professor of Political Science, George Rathjens, states:

. . . one could ask, "How many nuclear wars by the end of this century?" An answer must depend on how the world would react to that first nuclear war. My guess is that the first one will be relatively limited . . . . We have no way of predicting whether nuclear wars will become commonplace after one occurs or whether a first nuclear war will bring about a world reaction that may lead to major changes in political structure. In any case, I do think that a first nuclear war is probable and that it will involve large numbers of fatalities—tens or hundreds of thousands, perhaps millions, but not billions, although the kind of war that we and the Soviet Union could enter into could involve, certainly by the end of the century, fatalities on the order of at least a billion.

NUCLEAR WAR: OTHER CONSIDERATIONS

In assessing the chances of nuclear war there are some key points to consider. One is that the history of man is the history of war. Wars have been the rule, not the exception. Sean MacBride, a Nobel Peace Prize recipient and former President of the Council of Ministers of the Council of Europe, has devoted his life to international peace activities. He currently heads the International Peace Bureau, but notes with sadness that *all* the recent warnings by disarmament experts have fallen on deaf ears.[17]

Despite the pronouncements by what must be the last bastion of hopeful humanists, mankind has not changed essentially in its nature. Man is now, as he has always been, a basically selfish and prideful creature. In a world more complex than ever before, with increasingly more crises coming to a head, to say that man will now avoid war is to say that he will accomplish peace under the most stressful times of all history. The fact is that even under much more relaxed times in history, man always has gone to war.

The awful reality is that we are in a unique situation today. The well-being of the world demands that nuclear armaments *never* go off, and "never" is certainly a long time. Few people really *want* war, but we are ready for it and getting more ready every year.

In a relevant article entitled "Armageddon, Anyone?," Thomas Powers looks bleakly at the chances for peace. He makes the point, often pointed to by others, that until now the world's great armies have always gone to war sooner or later. The fleet of Darius the Great, the Roman Legions, the Spanish Armada, and so many more were all intended for war, and that is the activity for which they were ultimately used. We have no reason to believe that the present

situation should end any differently, even though we hope
that the end result will in fact be different. Powers makes
the point that we have had some sort of peace for 30 years,
but that there was peace of an even better sort for 42 years
between the Franco-Prussian War and the First World
War.[18]

We have already referred to Sean MacBride, and he
makes the truism that wars have been the rule rather than
the exception, and that they have become increasingly
worse and worse. The 1870 war was regarded very seriously
at the time, but in the light of present events, it was child's
play. Even the 1914 war was insignificant compared to
the last world war. MacBride makes the point that, "The
next will be the last."[19]

In the same context MacBride has some relevant comments about the weapons of atomic war. He realistically
points out that such weapons are unlikely to remain in silos
and never be used—that it would be sheer fantasy to believe the governments and men who now wield power are
more responsible than those of the past, or that there will
be no more "Hitlers" in our world. He points out that
there are 30 governments around the world enjoying democratic processes as we think of that term, but that there
are a hundred or so dictatorships. "Do we really believe
that there is no danger that some dictator will not use
these weapons?" MacBride points out that such problems
must be faced, and that everything else pales into insig-
nificance unless those problems are squarely met.

THE HISTORICAL PRECEDENT

Two of the saddest, yet most important, factors in
assessing our chances of nuclear war are, first, the historical fact that arms races have almost always ended in war
(a chance of 99.1%), and that 100% of those that did not,
ended in economic collapse for the countries involved.
The second factor is the absolute abundance of war in
man's history. According to Paul Doty of Harvard, about
30 million people died in wars between 1915 and 1945, not
including civil war deaths.[20]

Frank Barnaby is Director of the prestigious Stockholm International Peace Research Institute (SIPRI), and he has some relevant pointers regarding the subsequent years 1945 to 1975. He states that there have been activities that could be defined as war, either civil or international, 119 times between 1945 and 1975. If the total duration of those conflicts were added together they would exceed 350 years, and the territory of 69 countries, together with the armed forces of 81 states, were involved. Barnaby states that several tens of millions of people were killed in those wars, this being more than during World War II. He further tells us that since September, 1945, there has not been one single day in which there has not been one or more wars being fought somewhere in the world, with about 12 wars being waged on an "average" day. Barnaby makes the point that it is interesting to note the comparison in a list drawn up by an American scholar, Quincy Wright, who listed 24 wars taking place between 1900 and 1941. As Barnaby points out, "Whatever definition of war is used, however, there is general agreement that the frequency of war has increased and is still increasing."[21]

IN 55 CENTURIES, 292 YEARS OF PEACE

Even those figures do not tell the whole horrifying story. It is seen more clearly when computers are brought into the arena. A recent analysis from the *Stockton Herald* (California) tells of a survey utilizing an electronic computer, and finding that since 3600 B.C. the world has known only 292 years of peace. In that time stretching over more than 55 centuries there have been 14,531 wars in which over 3.6 billion people have been killed. Since 650 B.C. there have been 1,656 arms races and all except 16 of these ended in war and the other 16 ended in the economic collapse of the countries concerned.[22]

One final relevancy is the chance of nuclear war being started by self-fulfilling prophecy. Once it becomes acceptable that a nuclear war will in fact take place, such a happening may be inevitable. As Henry Kissinger has pointed out, the superpowers' attempt to hedge against every conceivable contingency actually fuels political tensions and "could well lead to a self-fulfilling prophecy."[23]

Frightening? Prophets of Doom? Or Realists? Some 2,500 years ago a man of God wrote about a time when men's flesh would rot while they stood on their feet, their eyes would rot in their sockets, and their tongues would dissolve in their mouths. It is written in the Old Testament, in Zechariah 14:12. The survivors of Hiroshima would not lightly dismiss that ancient "prophet of doom." Maybe in a special way he pointed to our own *Decade of Shock,* rushing upon us with relentless speed and certainty.

Footnotes: Chapter 2

1. J.E. Medalia, "The New Pentagon Strategy: Limited Nuclear War," *World Issues,* October-November, 1976, p. 14.
2. Sidney Lens, "The Arms Race: A Primer," *The Progressive,* October, 1977, p. 40.
3. Bernard T. Feld, "The Nuclear Dilemma Revisited," *The Bulletin of the Atomic Scientists,* February, 1977, p. 7.
4. "Peaceful Era in Space May Soon End," *The Futurist,* June, 1977, p. 191.
5. *Ibid.*
5a. *Ibid.*
6. Alfred Kastler, "The Challenge of the Century," *The Bulletin of the Atomic Scientists,* September, 1977, p. 20.
7. Frank Barnaby, "The Mounting Prospects of Nuclear War," *The Bulletin of the Atomic Scientists,* June, 1977, p. 13.
8. Note 6.

9. Bernard T. Feld, "The Charade of Piecemeal Arms Limitations," *Bulletin of the Atomic Scientists,* January, 1975, p. 8.
10. Carl Friedrich von Weizsacker, "On the Avoidance of Atomic War," *World Issues,* December, 1976-January, 1977, p. 3.
11. *Ibid.*
12. *Perspective,* July/August, 1976, p. 142 (book review).
13. Don Cook, "Nuclear War Specter Hangs Over The 1980's," *Los Angeles Times,* September 23, 1977.
14. Alfred Kastler, "The Challenge of The Century," *The Bulletin of the Atomic Scientists,* September, 1977, p. 21.
15. W.R. Van Cleave, S.T. Cohen, "Nuclear Aspects of Future U.S. Security Policy in Asia," *Orbis,* Fall, 1975; *Los Angeles Times,* November 25, 1977, part 1-B "U.S. Lacks Material For Conventional War."
16. "Nuclear War by 1999? Five Experts Think It Likely," *Current,* January, 1976, pp. 32-43.
17. Sean MacBride, "A New Morality for a New World," *The Bulletin of the Atomic Scientists,* September, 1977, p. 22.
18. Thomas Powers, "Armageddon, Anyone?" *Commonweal,* June 4, 1976, p. 369.
19. Sean MacBride, "A New Morality for a New World," *The Bulletin of the Atomic Scientists,* September, 1977, p. 22.
20. "Nuclear War by 1999?", *Current,* January, 1976, p. 34.
21. Frank Barnaby, "World Armament and Disarmament—A Report To The Stockholm International Peace Research Institute On The Growing Arsenals of War," *The Bulletin of the Atomic Scientists,* June, 1976, p. 25.
22. The Stockton Herald, Stockton, California. March 13-18, 1960, or March 3-8, 1963.
23. Henry Kissinger, "The Permanent Challenge of Peace: United States Policy Toward the Soviet Union," *The Atlantic Community Quarterly,* Spring, 1976, p. 28.

Chapter 3

Nuclear Terrorism

There are scores of terrorist groups around the world today. They include The Japanese Red Army, The PLO, Black September, The Weathermen, The Turkish People's Army, and there are others. Some qualified analysts are stating, "We are more likely to become casualties from nuclear terrorist attacks than from attacks by other countries."[1]

Mixing a volatile world with an abundance of plutonium will sooner or later produce a reaction of nuclear terrorism. Ours is an unstable world and as nuclear proliferation increases, there is the high probability of malevolent use of plutonium. David Rosenbaum put it clearly in the Winter, 1977 issue of *International Security:* "If strategic nuclear warfare between major nations is avoided, nuclear terrorism may be one of the most important political and social problems of the next fifty years."

In his terrifying book, *Brothers in Blood: The International Terrorist Network,* Ovid Demaris documents the existence of a dedicated international alliance of terrorists able to threaten us with a nuclear attack. Imagine the impact of a nuclear explosion on Capitol Hill during the State of the Union message. Impossible? The facts suggest otherwise. Terrorists are pragmatists. They have certain goals, and their activities to date show all too clearly that they will use any means to achieve them.

A typical example involved State Senator John V. Briggs who was warned by the FBI in October of 1977 that he had been targeted by the terrorist "weather underground" as an assassination victim. Five members of the group were arrested just hours before the attempt: they had planned to open a campaign of bombing and assassination of public officials. According to an undercover agent, two members told him, "They planned to kill both public officials and private individuals who opposed their revolutionary objectives."[2] Italy's Red Brigades did just this to Aldo Moro.

BLOW UP AIRPLANES "IN FLIGHT WHEN OUR TARGET IS THERE"

The West German Badder-Meinhof guerrilla group recently warned it would blow up airplanes, "In flight when our target is there. We shall act everywhere . . . . "[3] Senator Abraham Ribicoff, calling terrorism an "ongoing and continuous war," stated, "No one is safe today. There isn't a person in any country that is safe from terrorism." He noted that between 1968 and 1975 there were 913 international terrorist incidents that affected U.S. citizens, and "cited a CIA report which said there was a 79% chance for terrorists to escape punishment and death, and an absolute certainty they would get publicity."[4]

Interestingly, he cited Libya as the Number 1 training ground for terrorists in the world today. Its President is known to be less than stable and to be hopeful of soon obtaining or making nuclear weapons. Palestinian guerrillas have demonstrated that both nuclear fuel and tactical nuclear bombs are vulnerable to raids by disciplined terrorists, and the 7,000 nuclear warheads the U.S. keeps in Europe are one possible target. Even the Mafia could attempt the nuclear blackmail of a government for some political or economic gain.

People in general refuse to think that "it" could ever

happen—that apart from anything else, security would see that it didn't. However, the facts are not so comforting. Daniel Yergin notes: "Physical security is never perfect. Not so long ago a lunatic walked unnoticed into the control room of a French nuclear plant and randomly threw several switches before being detected. Such a danger is so real that in the United States guards now have shoot-to-kill orders at fourteen federal nuclear installations."[5]

The *Defense Monitor* is a highly regarded publication of the Center for Defense Information in Washington D.C., and in a recent issue it reported that U.S. Army Special Forces exercises have demonstrated that nuclear weapons storage areas can be successfully penetrated without being detected despite the presence of guards, fences, and sensors. The point they are making is that if this can be done by Special Forces detecting such a possibility, it obviously could be done also by a daring and well-organized terrorist organization.[6]

If nuclear terrorists do manage to seize nuclear weapons, the situation could be totally catastrophic. David Rosenbaum, writing in *International Security,* presents a scenario involving a terrorist group who sends a letter to the White House stating nuclear bombs have been hidden in three of the largest cities in the U.S. and will be exploded unless their demands are met. The demands are (1) that the U.S. must immediately renounce all defense and security agreements; (2) that the U.S. must pull back all overseas troops and equipment within 6 months and cease all arms sales; (3) fifty billion dollars a year must be turned over to Third World countries via the U.N.; (4) all minority prisoners must be released from all federal prisons within three months; (5) USS Armed Forces must be reduced to 75,000 within a year.

The problem in this scenario is that nothing can be done—can we evacuate the cities without terrorists setting off the bombs? If the demands are ignored, tens of millions of innocent people may die. On the other hand, in the thinking of the terrorists tens of millions die every year anyway, from famines, disease, war, accidents, and so on.

The other side of the coin is, if the demands *are* met, what will stop more demands? Where does it all end? Or should we say, *when* will it all end? Will we ever get through *The Decade of Shock?*

What nuclear terrorism means is that a nation of over 200 million and all its military might has the choice either to bow before a small group of radicals or to suffer the cost.

NUCLEAR ENERGY AND SECURITY

Some people do not believe that civil liberties and the extensive use of nuclear power are compatible: they believe nuclear energy will require security measures that will turn America into a garrison State.

This is one of the obvious solutions to preventing terrorism, and clearly nuclear terrorism could tend to push a country toward dictatorship. As terrorist acts increase, so do the calls for centralized law and order, restriction of freedom (to punish offenders and to insure order), etc.

What is certain is that there will be military violence in countries with large nuclear industries, and it is also certain that there are no guaranteed safeguards against nuclear terror in a world of malfunctioning people. In any case, the U.S. safeguards are inadequate to begin with, and the problem is a worldwide concern.[7] It is a problem bigger than just any one country.

It is indicative of the signs of our times that at a late 1976 meeting of over 200 experts from 55 countries, discussing the problems of the North-South regions (the rich and poor countries), "Many participants feared that it might take a major crisis, or outright chaos, or nuclear blackmail, to motivate the developed countries to engage jointly in global income distribution, however modest."[8]

Not only individual groups, but countries also might participate in nuclear terror or blackmail. Some countries are more terrorist-oriented than others, obvious examples being Uganda and Libya. It is entirely believable that in the foreseeable future their evil leaders could use nuclear bombs to back up their demands for any conceivable number of bizarre operations.

Another very real possibility is that countries in which the U.S. has nuclear arsenals may turn around and seize the bombs, perhaps at the insistence of another country that is in turn threatening them with obliteration.

"TERRORIZE OPPONENTS INTO ACQUIESCENCE"

Unfortunately, many countries in the world today give asylum to terrorists. A recent Library of Congress study included the following nations as being so involved: The Soviet Union, China, North Korea, Cuba, Libya, Algeria, Syria, South Yemen, Iraq, Lebanon, Tanzania, the Congo, Zaire. These countries not only give terrorists asylum, but they actively aid and support them.[9] The USSR, for example, has openly recognized the terrorist PLO as a legitimate political organization and has given them sophisticated weapons and training. The obvious and not so obvious risks and bizarre opportunities are frightening to contemplate.

For Communist countries this is nothing new: Marx' ideals were, in his own words: "The disarming of the bourgeoisie . . . revolutionary terror . . . and the creation of a revolutionary army. [The new revolutionary Government would] have neither time nor opportunity for compassion or remorse. Its business is to terrorize its opponents into acquiescence. It must disarm antagonism by execution, imprisonment, forced labor, control of the press . . . . "[10] It is all too clear that, apart from internation cooperation, terrorism will continue.

On the other hand, Dr. Petr Beckman, in *The Health Hazards of Not Going Nuclear,* presents some opposing arguments which decrease somewhat the likelihood of terrorist nuclear activity.[11] One of them is defensive infiltration of terrorist organizations, an option which he notes has been all but destroyed by "liberals" in Congress decrying "loss of civil liberties" (which is not the case). Another factor is the risk that terrorists take to get the bombs. Dr. Bernard Cohen points out there is a 50% death risk in stealing a bomb and a 30% risk in making one.[12]

It is relevant to note in passing that homemade nuclear bombs generally would kill thousands, not millions, but that stolen high quality nuclear bombs would be a quite different matter. Both Beckman and Cohen point out that there are many methods terrorists could use which are far more destructive than nuclear bombs. The blowing up of hydroelectric dams around the country could kill millions. Blowing up a ship carrying liquid natural gas could have the effect of a Hiroshima-type bomb in a large port city. Distributing superlethal nerve gas over a city when wind conditions were right is another dreadful possibility. As Dr. Cohen notes: "A large, well led, heavily armed group of terrorists, striking at a time and place of their choosing, can commit as much mass murder as suits their purpose, and no amount of guarding or police action can stop them."[13]

Terrorists have had these options for some time and have not yet used them, either because they have some concept of morality left or because they would thereby gather no public sympathy. To utilize such an option might even call down on themselves universal contempt, and this would seriously hamper their cause.

TERRORIST BLACKMAIL
MUST BE REJECTED

Both the above-quoted authorities also agree (as we, the authors, do) that the surest way to decrease or even stop terrorist activity is to *not* give in to them. Cohen states: "But if terrorists should decide to employ mass murder there can be only one answer: Society must learn to not yield to blackmail. To yield is to live under constant tyranny, whereas to stand fast is a guarantee of eventual victory."[14]

Beckman states:

> The PLO and other organizations that kill indis-
> criminately have blackmailed their murderers out
> of prison in all concerned countries except one:

Israel. Israel has, from the beginning, not merely proclaimed that it will not negotiate with black-mailers, but it has stood by its word, and the terrorists have given up on kidnapping Israeli citizens or otherwise trying to blackmail the Israeli government.[15]

He notes that West European governments have general-ly given in to terrorist demands, to save a few lives *now* but resulting in thousands being sacrificed later.

Unfortunately, we do face the possibility that terrorists will become so frustrated and angry that they may resort to things they have never attempted before. A report pre-pared for the Nuclear Regulatory Commission of the MITRE Corporation, written by twelve top experts on terrorism and sabotage, stated that such a possibility "should be taken very seriously." "Terrorist groups may find themselves in political situations where they feel they have nothing to lose by an act, no matter how outra-geous . . . . "[16] The report noted that if such an act were directed against the U.S. it might even make them heroes to a substantial segment of the world.

TERRORISM IN THE MIDDLE EAST

Louis Rene Beres, Professor of Political Science at Purdue University, is another who warns against terrorist activities. He states: "With more than 50 major terrorist groups operating in the world, many in The Middle East, terrorist activity may well lead to nuclear destruction."[17] He makes several important observations:

1. There is growing cooperation among terrorists around the world.
2. This enhances their chances of acquiring nuclear ma-terial.
3. They are willing to die, and some have done so de-liberately: some members of the Popular Front for the Liberation of Palestine (PFLP) will "often in-tentionally detonate their explosive-crammed belts on the completion of a mission."

4. Middle East groups have an attitude of total war against ethnic groups, religions, and nations, and their anger is vented randomly—the killing of Israeli athletes, school children, hotel occupants, and airport passengers. As Professor Beres states, "The Palestinian terrorists have no inhibitions against the application of maximum force to virtually any segment of human population other than their own."

Beres concludes by stating that apart from real international cooperation, which is something lacking at the present, "The threat of nuclear terrorism is very real." He warns that, "Unless the possibility of terrorist use of nuclear weapons is quickly eliminated, there may be immeasureable calamity in the Middle East."

Footnotes: Chapter 3

1. L.R. Beres, "Terrorism And The Nuclear Threat In The Middle East," *Current History,* January, 1976, p. 27.
2. *Los Angeles Times,* November 20, 1977.
3. *Los Angeles Times,* November 20, 1977.
4. *Los Angeles Times,* October 25, 1977.
5. Daniel Yergin, "The Terrifying Prospect: Atomic Bombs Everywhere," *Atlantic Monthly,* April, 1977, p. 56.
6. Louis R. Beres, "Terrorism And The Nuclear Threat In The Middle East," *Current History,* January, 1976, p. 27, citing the *Defense Monitor,* Vol. 4, No. 2, p. 8.
7. D.D. Comey, "The Perfect Trojan Horse," *The Bulletin of the Atomic Scientists,* June, 1976, p. 33.
8. Andre Van Dam, "Hope For The World's Neediest People?", *The Futurist,* August, 1977, p. 224.

9. *Los Angeles Times,* October 25, 1977.
10. Harold J. Luski, *Karl Marx: An Essay* (London: The Fabrian Society, 1925), pp. 19, 39.
11. Petr Beckman, *The Health Hazards Of Not Going Nuclear,* (Boulder, Colorado: The Golem Press) 1976.
12. Bernard Cohen, "The Potentialities of Terrorism," *Bulletin of the Atomic Scientists,* June, 1976, p. 35.
13. *Ibid.*
14. *Ibid.*
15. Petr Beckman, *The Health Hazards Of Not Going Nuclear,* pp. 146-7.
16. D.O. Comey, "The Perfect Trojan Horse," *The Bulletin of the Atomic Scientists,* June, 1976, p. 33.
17. L. R. Beres, "Terrorism And The Nuclear Threat In The Middle East," *Current History,* January, 1976, p. 27.

Chapter 4

Supremacy Whittled Away

One of the great deterrents to nuclear war has been the clear supremacy of the United States over Russia in many significant areas. However, that supremacy is being whittled away rapidly.

The pendulum has swung dramatically, and at some points the balance of power is no longer with the West. Henry Kissinger wrote in 1976 that as late as 1962 the United States had a five-to-one superiority in strategic missiles, a three-to-one superiority in strategic bombers, entire Naval superiority everywhere, and approximate equality on the ground in Europe.[1] One result was that the Russians backed down at the time of the Cuban missile crisis in 1962, but since then it has been a different story.

The fact is that the Soviet Union has emerged as a first class military power, especially because of her dramatic developments in the field of nuclear technology. Now they are on approximately equal terms with the United States, so far as their strategic military potential is concerned.

Kissinger further states: "For the first time in history the Soviet Union can threaten distant places beyond the Eurasian land-mass—including the United States. With no part of the world outside the range of its military forces, the USSR has begun to define its interests and objectives in global terms. Soviet diplomacy has thrust into the Middle East, Africa, and Asia. This evolution is now rooted in real power, rather than a rhetorical manifestation of a universalist doctrine which in fact has very little validity or appeal.''

SOVIET SACRIFICES— AND SUPPRESSION

While it may be true that Soviet doctrine "has very little validity or appeal," it is also true that the Soviets have deliberately imposed great sacrifices on both their "own" people and those brought within their immediate influence, with the clear-cut goal of achieving a military strength that would be unchallengeable. One undoubted result is the serious whittling away of U.S. supremacy.

Not the least of the Russian advantages is that they are not a democracy. If it suits their objective, they can suppress information—and they can suppress people. The rulers rule, and outside the inner circle they condone little questioning of their decisions and actions. They do not need to fear that a Congress will insist on restraints once decisions have been made, as was the embarrassing situation for U.S. military leaders at the time of the blatant Russian activity in the Angola affair. In the United States there has been a constant demand for defense budgets to be revised, to the delight of Soviet watchers.

So far as the democracies are concerned, all is not lost by any means. As Kissinger puts it, "It is the great industrial democracies, not the Soviet Union, that are the engine of the world economy, and the most promising partners for the poorer nations." Soviet power is essentially military, and its economic resources are not equal to those of the Western democracies. Nor is it able to offer the network of medical, scientific, and humanitarian help that the United States and other democracies can offer to a world that is terrified by the very real threat of a nuclear holocaust, a calamity that could annihilate hundreds of millions of people around the world in just a few days.

This is not idle talk or wild exaggeration. Our coming

Decade of Shock is likely to be different from all previous decades in a number of ways. Another result of the whittling away of U.S. supremacy is that more than one country now has horrifically destructive weapons that can cover almost unlimited distances, virtually instantaneously. The whole world, literally, is in constant peril of a nuclear holocaust, beside which Hiroshima would seem small indeed.

"EACH SIDE WOULD LOSE AT LEAST 100 MILLION"

No longer is the U.S. the unchallenged world military leader, and the two major powers (U.S. and Russia) are lined up, each watching the other as terrifying know-how in horror technology increases. Neither can allow the other to get ahead too far, for, as Kissinger points out in that same article, each side would lose at least 100 million in a nuclear exchange. Assumptions that one side could avoid such catastrophic conditions would depend on the other side not launching its missiles before the missile silos themselves were destroyed. That is unthinkable, and, in fact, all parties to a nuclear holocaust would themselves face virtual extinction. There could be no winners.

DANGEROUS COMMUNICATION BREAKDOWNS

The ultimate decision for nuclear attack is with the President, and that decision could be called for, with the briefest of notice, at any time of the day or night. Where is U.S. supremacy in the event of a communications breakdown?

That little button might well be pushed at a time of misinterpretation (or even non-receipt) of intelligence data. In the *L.A. Times* of November 24, 1977, Greg Rushford has a report headed "U.S. Military Communications Vulnerable." He quotes a House Investigating Subcommittee in regard to communications problems. He elaborates the poor communications during the 1964 Gulf of Tonkin crisis. At that time the destroyer *Maddox* had such trouble sending reports to higher commands (via relay stations in the Philippines and Hawaii) that the White House was not really sure what was happening off Vietnam. Rushford further states, "Three years later, during the Six-Day War in 1967, the Pentagon tried and failed for over 13 hours to contact the USS *Liberty,* on patrol off the Sinai Peninsula, to order it out of the danger zone. The messages were not received, and the ship was fired upon by the Israelis. It turned out that messages from Washington had been directed, apparently through clerical errors, to naval communications stations in the Philippines and Morocco, and to the National Security Agency, which directs technical intelligence missions from Ft. Meade, MD.

Similar communications problems were linked with the *Pueblo* incident of 1968 (when that ship was seized by the North Koreans) and the shooting down of an ED-121 spy plane over North Korea in 1969.

With all the sophistication available to the West, human error and technological breakdown plague us and could lead to that dreaded holocaust we all hope isn't just over the edge of our horizon. Traditional U.S. communications supremacy, real or imagined, is completely whittled away when even in simpler spheres of communication there are almost incredible areas of nonsophistication. Interception of military communications was relatively common during the Vietnam War, but as late as February, 1977 the House Armed Services Committee was issuing this warning (we quote from Rushford):

> The record clearly establishes an urgent need for a greatly enhanced, secure voice capability at both the strategic and tactical levels of command and control.

In view of all this it is relevant to ask, "Is the U.S. still the greatest military power on earth?" The answer is, "Yes," but beset by human weaknesses and inherent technological deficiencies that could all too soon cause it to be written, "It *was* the greatest military power on earth."

THE BUILDUP ACCELERATES

Some time ago there was an interesting series of cartoons. One man (we'll call him A) was whispering to another man (B), and surreptitiously A was pointing to a third man (C). As a result B bought a small handgun from A. Then A went to C, whispered about B, and C bought a bigger gun. Now it was back to B, then to C, over to B again—and soon B and C had each bought a huge stockpile of weapons in their determination to be stronger than the other. The first man A made huge profits, and the people dependent on B and C were called on to make great sacrifices so that B and C could increase their armaments and A could get rich.

On an international scale, the same thing has happened in our day. Facts and figures as to the cost of preparations come from highly reputable sources. One example is from the Congressional Record of January 30, 1976. Defense Secretary Donald H. Rumsfeld presented his report to the House Armed Services Committee and stated that, to offset the Soviet threat, the President was recommending increases running into billions of dollars. Some of the proposed additions were $2.9 billion for the Navy's Trident submarine, $1.5 billion for the Air Force B-1 bomber, $84 million to explore the land-based MX missile, and $262 million to accelerate development of long-range cruise missiles. The total proposed was $9.4 billion for 1977, compared with $7.3 billion for 1976.

SOVIET MILITARY SPENDING
GREATER THAN U.S.A.'S

That is a huge increase in a military budget, but the Soviet Union is reported to spend even more (in real money terms) on its military budget—comparative figures for the years 1963 to 1973 are given by Fred C. Ikle, an expert on world military expenditures. He is Director of the U.S. Arms Control and Disarmament Agency. His report is in *Armed Forces Journal International* of March, 1975. The figures given are based on what the Soviet spending would cost at United States prices: they show a 27% increase in the Soviet defense budget, with an increase of only 4% in constant dollars for the United States over the same period. ("Constant" dollars are the value of the expenditure based on 1973 figures.)

The report elaborated three other significant trends, these being:

1. The developing nations are devoting an increasing percentage of their gross national product to military spending.
2. The United States continues to maintain its role as the top exporter of arms.
3. The estimated annual value of the arms trade around the world continues to rise and has doubled from $4.4 billion in 1963 to $8.7 billion in 1973.

The bulk of the rise in expenditure was in the trouble spots of the Middle East and Southeast Asia.

The trends are alarming, and today experts are speaking out, warning of the danger and urging against short-sightedness. An example is in a speech by Thomas C. Reed, Secretary of the United States Air Force, delivered at the University Club at San Diego on April 30, 1976. Reed talks about wise decisions in the Nation's past, and asks questions about the future:

> Do we have the determination, the foresight, the will, to remain free for another 100 years?

> To chart a safe course in the years ahead we must recognize the recent emergency of alarming trends that could jeopardize our future security.

> Fourteen years ago the world saw the first major confrontation between nuclear superpowers—
> the Cuban Missile Crisis. Those six days of October, 1962, brought the world to the brink of nuclear war. A steadfast national determination,

backed up by overwhelming U.S. strategic superiority, let us deal with the situation from a
position of strength.[2]

Reed goes on to survey the events that followed: President Kennedy expressed the hope that the governments of
the world could turn their attention to ending the arms
race and reducing world tension, but "in fact the Soviet
arms buildup was about to begin."

NO LONGER "PRIMITIVE" POWER!

We have said that the Soviets are not restricted by
policy changes and the necessity to electioneer. Within two
years of the Cuba missiles threat, Kruschev was deposed
and the more technology-minded pair of Brezhnev and
Kosygin replaced him. Since that time Russian defense
resources have increased by at least three per cent each
year, without retrenchments, distractions, or adjustments
of priorities, and without public debate or dissent. As
Thomas C. Reed pointed out, "The momentum continues
to be both obvious and ominous."

The facts that follow in Reed's speech are frightening.
From 1965 to 1976, the Soviet rocket force increased from
225 Intercontinental Ballistic Missiles to about 1600;
Soviets achieved a four-to-one weight advantage with
Minuteman missiles; from being essentially a coastal
defense force, the Soviet Navy has become a first class
Navy with over 1,300 ships; they have come from having
a few dozen primitive submarine ballistic missiles launch
tubes to the position where they are now a major force,
having 730 submarine launch tubes, with nuclear submarines. Strategic warheads and bombs have increased
from 450 to 2,500, and 2,000 tactical aircraft have been
added to the Soviet forces. Reed further tells us that in
the last three years the Soviets have produced almost six
times as many tanks, three times as many armored personnel carriers, and nine times as many artillery pieces as
the U.S., and 70 percent more tactical aircraft.

The world has not seen such a rapid peacetime military

buildup since the German rearmament of the 1930's.

As we read on, we find some startling facts from Thomas Reed's speech. He warns that the United States Air Force aircraft inventory is down by more than one-third from what it was in 1968, to a present figure of about 9,200 planes. In actual numbers of aircraft, that is the lowest it has been since 1950, which was immediately prior to the Korean War. In the 10 years prior to his speech (1976) the U.S. had built less than 300 ships but had retired over 800, and so there were less than 500 ships in the nation's active fleet. The last time the U.S. had that few ships was in 1939.

The Decade of Shock is about to hit us. Reed's article leads to that: "Even the one compensating factor we have enjoyed in years past, technological superiority, could slip away if we are not careful. The Director of Defense Research and Engineering, Dr. Malcolm Currie, recently warned that continuation of present trends could lead to dominance by the Soviet Union in deployed military technology in the 1980's."

SAIGON REMINDS US THAT A
NUCLEAR WAR MAY NOT BE NECESSARY

The fact is, a nuclear war may not be necessary for the achievement of Soviet aims. Reed puts the point well:

Will all this growth of weaponry lead to a nuclear Armageddon? Of course not, for the same reason that Saigon was not burned to the ground a year ago. There was no need. At the end, tanks were as decisive in South Vietnam as ICBM's are on the world scene. When the North Vietnamese were able to concentrate enough firepower around the city, the conflict was all over. The advent of modern information systems means that both sides can now count quickly and accurately. The North Vietnamese put a few shells onto the Tan Son Nhut runway to signal the end, and the South Vietnamese had no choices left—a classic of modern coercion.

Alexander Solzhenitsyn is quoted as saying in New York in the summer of 1975:

> There is no guarantee for anything in the West. You want to believe otherwise, so you cut down your armies, you cut down your research. But believe me, the Soviet Union is not cutting down anything.

> Soon they will be twice as powerful as you, and then five times, and then ten times. And some day they will say to you: "We are marching our troops into Western Europe and if you act, we shall annihilate you." And the troops will move, and you will not act.[3]

Reed tells us that each of the TRIAD units needs modernization: "For the past 6 years our national defense strategy has been securely anchored by a credible Triad of strategic forces. Modernization of each leg of that strategic Triad now is essential—it is our best insurance for peace in America's third century."

A TAKEN-FOR-GRANTED ADVANTAGE

What happens if all this continues and the United States loses its TRIAD superiority?—a superiority involving land-based ICBM's, ballistic missiles from submarines, and air-borne nuclear weapons. The fleet of 41 Polaris and Poseidon submarines reach the end of their acceptable service lives in the decade we are entering[4] and the B-52 bombers are 14 years old. After initial proposals of cutbacks, there is now an accelerated program for ICBM improvement. The Soviets have a superiority in numbers of ICBM's (1600 to 1000), and they took no similar action when the United States temporarily suspended production. As stated elsewhere, the Soviets now have a numerical advantage of 4 to 1. The United States is rushing into intensified reprogramming and production.

In contrast to the restraints on U.S. developments, Soviet modernization efforts are of unsurpassed magnitude. They feature four new ICBM families, all with greater payload capacities than their predecessors, and all being tested with MIRV's (*M*ultiple *I*ndependently targeted *R*eentry *V*ehicle).

Here are some other frightening facts from Daniel Graham's article in the *Armed Forces Journal International* of April, 1976. (Graham is the recently-retired Director of the Defense Intelligence Agency.)

> America's strategic defensive plans include no procurement and extensive cutbacks. All anti-ballistic missiles will be removed this year. All six Air National Guard F-101 interceptor squadrons will phase out by the end of FY 1977, partly because of budgetary priorities, partly because of beliefs that "without effective ABM defenses, air defenses are of limited value against aggressors armed primarily with strategic missiles."

> Soviet strength is growing rapidly in Central Europe, according to recent statements by the Chairman of NATO's Military Committee.

> As it stands, the quantitative balance continues to shift toward the Soviet Union. U.S. qualitative superiority never compensated completely and, in certain respects, is slowly slipping away. America's global responsibilities, coupled with U.S. reliance on reserve components, permit the Soviet Union to concentrate power while we remain dispersed, depending heavily on allies and arms control accords to safeguard our national interests.

> Some of the cogent U.S. shortcomings, identified in earlier sections would lose significance if this

country scaled down its overseas interests, accepting uncertain costs related to reduced world power status, the possible loss of Free World leadership, and long-range U.S. security.

Another article in the *Armed Forces Journal International* (July, 1975) warns that the Soviet submarine threat is now 10 times that from Germany at the time World War II broke out. The capacity to counter this Soviet threat is correspondingly smaller, with approximately a tenth as many antisubmarine escort ships in ratio to enemy submarines as were used by the British and U.S. forces in World War II.

This information came from Senator Robert Taft of Ohio, in speeches to the U.S. Senate. The Soviet Union had at that time (1975) about 340 submarines to 115 by U.S.A. The U.S. has 99 destroyers and 66 other escort vessels—2 Russian subs for each antisubmarine escort ship. For each German U-boat in World War II there were 25 British and U.S. warships and 100 aircraft. According to Senator Taft, quoting from Admiral of the Fleet, Sergei Gorshkov, for every German submarine at sea there were 100 British and American antisubmarines. The ratios given are actually unrealistic by today's standards, for nuclear subs have far greater capacities than the diesel-powered subs of World War II. Nevertheless, conventional weapons of great numerical superiority could not fully limit even those subs.

Added to this (Senator Taft reported) is the prospect of the Soviets launching over 1,400 antiship missiles simultaneously. That represents 100 Soviet missiles against each U.S. carrier, and "The United States still has not deployed any antiship missiles." Russia has over 140 fast missile boats, China has about 80, and the U.S. has two, with two more being built.

SOME SOVIET ECONOMIC ADVANTAGES

Even in economic matters the U.S. supremacy has been whittled away to a certain extent. The Soviets have a tremendous advantage in some economic areas, for their country is relatively self-sufficient in raw materials, much of which must be imported by the United States. Also, their pay scales are drastically lower, and their expected standards of living are much lower than is to be found in the United States. In addition, their production potential is much greater per capita than in this country.

Pay and allowances absorb 53% of the U.S. defense budget, and related costs, such as housing, push the cost to nearly 65 cents of each dollar. As Daniel Graham puts it in the article referred to above: "The Soviet Union, with far lower pay scales and a controlled economy less afflicted by inflation, could afford a larger force and modernize at a more rapid rate if its total defense budget were exactly the same as that of the United States."

THEN THERE ARE THE MARINES . . . .

Another sphere of contrast is with the Merchant Marines. In the main, the United States depends on privately operated ships whose alien crews owe no allegiance to the United States. The Soviet Merchant Marine, by contrast, consists mainly of modern, highly automated ships that currently carry more than half of all the Kremlin's transoceanic cargo. Coordination with the Soviet Navy is complete.

In another area Daniel Graham gives us an optimistic note, for the U.S. is superior in its strength of amphibious landing forces: several Army divisions as well as three Marine divisions are also qualified in this area. Graham reminds us that U.S. carrier air power is available from the Marines as well as the Navy, and the U.S. edge is absolute.

As we go on we shall see that there are other factors. Our chapters are not actually self-contained and there is necessarily a measure of overlap. It would be equally convincing to put some statements in one chapter instead of another, for there is startling material that is as relevant to one of our chosen sections as to another. The more we study the material, the more it becomes obvious that the "taken-for-granted" supremacy of the United States has indeed been whittled away.

The time for reassessment has forced itself upon us, and even now it might be past. The Decade of Shock might show that we took inventory too late.

Footnotes: Chapter 4

1. See Chapter 2, note 23.
2. *Vital Speeches Of The Day,* Vol. 42, No. 18, July 1, 1976. p. 548.
3. For a similar quote from a different lecture see Solzhenitsyn, *Warning to the West,* p. 77.
4. Reed, *op. cit.,* note 2.

Chapter 5

HOW THE WEST WAS ~~WON~~ LOST!

The very nature of its government control means that the Soviets would be better prepared for nuclear war than Americans. Daniel Graham further reports:

> Some studies in fact claim that city evacuation plans shortly will enable the Soviets to engage in nuclear combat with far fewer casualties than this country. That contention is unconfirmed, but even partial defenses could buttress the Kremlin's bargaining power in times of intense international crisis by undercutting our second-strike Assured Destruction threat.[1]

When France withdrew from military participation in NATO, a dramatic change soon developed in the actual placing of American supplies. Daniel Graham comments:

> Some U.S. aircraft and logistical installations were repositioned in the United Kingdom, but most U.S. supplies, including ammunition, are stored within a 30-mile radius of Kaiserslautenn. The first sharp Soviet surge could sever friendly supply lines, which radiate from Bremerhaven,

Rotterdam, and Antwerp, then run closely behind and parallel to the prospective front. Air-
fields could also be overrun. Every lucrative
military target, including command/control centers, air bases, ports, and supply depots is
within easy reach of Soviet IRBM's and
MRBM's.

UN-FREE BUT UNITED

Such problems can be multiplied, for the "Allies"
are by no means as united as the "Un-Free" forces
behind the Iron Curtain. On the European front it is
recognized that Portugal is politically unstable, and that
Italy has its own serious economic and political problems.
Greece and Turkey are more concerned about each other
than the nations of the Warsaw Pact, and France would
participate in action with the "Allies" only if its leaders
considered their own nation's interests would thus be best
served.

If troops had to be available in a hurry could a sea-
lift be effective in time? Daniel Graham's authoritative
comment is that it is in fact an improbability. He estimates that it would take two months for a Marine
amphibious force of one division with its air wing to be
involved in an amphibious assault. Whether such operations could succeed under general war conditions is con-
tentious.

There are other problems faced by the Allies that the
Russians do not face. Duplication and lack of standardization has decreased the effective force of NATO
by about 30%.[2] This increases annual costs by about
$11.2 billion (i.e., $11,200,000,000). That is a lot of tax-
payers' money to throw away because of nonplanning
or nonagreement.

Where does it all end? In a hellish holocaust whereby
man demonstrates his devilish potential to destroy all
mankind? Or does it point the way to a world dictator?

It is a truism that coming events cast their shadows.

Another pointer was the Angola affair, which was of tremendous importance in a number of ways. One was that it made clear that the Soviets could depend on the United States Congress to be very slow in further military incursions. For whatever reasons, there was no continuing taste for another Vietnam, even if human rights were seriously violated. Angola demonstrated that the United States had given up its historic and expected role of World Policeman.

It was of great importance also because, for the first time, the Soviet Union moved great distances to impose its own regime by military action. Millions of dollars worth of equipment and some 11,000 Cuban combat troops were utilized, and the daring Soviet strategy was successful. It was a first for Russia, and a first against the United States. For the first time it allowed the Russians to make violating movements outside Russia's own immediate recognized sphere of influence. Congress made it abundantly clear that it would not approve U.S. intervention.

AN OMINOUS PRECEDENT —
NO RESISTANCE

The danger for the world is in the ominous precedent that was thereby set. Russia had challenged, had met no strong American resistance, and so had gained tremendous confidence for the next moves in a deadly chess game in which the nations of the world are but pawns. Continued Congressional pressures against American involvement have further strengthened Russian hands, and lessened the desire for diplomatic settlement on the part of the Russians.[3]

It is wishful thinking to hope that local people (such as the Africans over the Angola issue) will eventually see the folly of accepting Russian domination. It is no good shutting the gate after the horse has bolted, and the escalations that have already taken place in this decade can well be likened to a galloping horse.

The divisions relating to American policies are paralyzing this nation's potential to ensure peace. What must one more decade bring? So far we have seen only the beginnings of the effects of increased potential.

EVIDENCE FOR RUSSIAN DECEIT

We cannot take comfort in the hope that the Soviets will respect agreements made in good faith. When it suits them, those agreements will be metaphorically torn up, at a moment's notice.

The evidence for Russian deceit has been aired in various places. Alexander Solzhenitsyn's *Warning To The West* (1976) is a book that should have wide circulation, discussing as it does overall Russian strategy for destroying the West. "The Case Against Kissinger" is a good example. It is an editorial in *Aviation Week and Space Technology* of December 8, 1975, based on testimony given before the House Select Committee on Intelligence and the Senate Foreign Relations Committee. The article assesses evidence given by the former Chief of Naval Operations, Admiral Elmo Zumwalt, and by former Defense Secretary James Schlessinger.

According to this editorial, Zumwalt and Schlessinger both confirmed many of the accusations that had been made concerning Soviet violations of the SALT agreement. In the same issue of *Aviation Week* it was claimed that Kissinger had withheld information about violations from President Ford, from Congress, and from military intelligence officials.

Zumwalt is quoted as telling Congress that the Soviets cheated on basic SALT agreements in three clear and precise forms, as follows:

> Interference with national means of verification and detection, testing of the SA-5 radar in the ABM mode, and deployment of a new phased-array SA-5-type radar for long-range detection in Kamchatka.

In this chapter we are not dealing with "the Kissinger question," but we are touching it in passing only insofar as it relates to our major theme. It is opposed to our basic culture to condone deception as an accepted pattern of thinking and planning. In practice there is a great deal of deceit, but treaties and agreements are taken seriously as bilateral covenants that should be respected.

This highlights one aspect of the serious problems facing the democracies when it comes to strategic planning and decision making, for those opposing us all too often regard such compliance as weakness. Zumwalt criticized the role of Kissinger as Chairman of the SALT Verification Committee, after being removed as Head of the National Security Council. It became clear that there had not been a shift in power, and we shall see that this is highly relevant.

In that same issue of *Aviation Week* Clarence A. Robinson writes:

> Zumwalt said that in his last month in office, before former President Nixon went to Moscow in 1974, he wrote a 12-page letter to the President expressing his concerns over Soviet SALT violations.

> "It had reached the point where we were just about ready," Zumwalt said, "as the Executive Branch, to face up to the question of Soviet cheating, but we were still dealing with it within the Executive Branch."

The charges made against Kissinger are highly relevant to our theme, on at least two major grounds. First, there was deception on the part of the Russian authorities, and they "got away with it" for a considerable period of time.

INTELLIGENCE NOT INFORMED

Secondly, after the deception was known, they were not confronted with the evidence, and even after Kissinger had investigated certain loopholes, for an extensive period he kept information secret from the intelligence personnel involved. Kissinger is quoted as ordering former Defense Secretary Schlessinger not to submit certain information from the Joint Chiefs of Staff summit meeting of June-July, 1974. Zumwalt bluntly claimed that he suspected Kissinger of not wanting to send it, rather than that the President was not wanting to receive it.

Zumwalt is further quoted in the same article: "But the most important fact is that for months the intelligence community had been denied the most valid explanation of what the Soviets were up to with regard to their development of the KY-9 or, as it later became known, SS-NX-13, a new, modern ballistic missile which would have qualified for deployment in diesel submarines under the badly flawed White House agreement."

Information kept from a President . . . secret agreements by an individual . . . cheating in regard to treaties kept from Intelligence . . . serious breaches that open the door to enemy strategic superiority of a frightening order, yet "pigeon-holed" by one high government official. If the charges are true, the prospects for a secure peace are not very encouraging.

We are already beginning to experience the birth-pains of *The Decade of Shock*. Those accusations against Kissinger touch only one aspect, but it is certainly a serious one. We are not thinking so much of the man but of the frightening power that can be wrongly used by one man with enormous authority. It is seen as a fact of life with Kissinger's actions in relation to the SALT agreement.

Not the least serious aspect is the "Pandora's Box" in the area of intelligence. To quote Zumwalt again:

> The most worrisome aspect of SALT violations by the Soviets has been the increasing Soviet interference with U.S. intelligence collection.

> But let me state publicly that in my judgment there have been significant violations of the SALT 1 agreements by the Soviets in their in-

terference with our national means of detection which have produced a serious reduction in our ability to check against Soviet cheating. This interference makes it easier for the Soviets to claim they are not cheating, harder for the U.S. to prove they are, and is, in and of itself, the most positive indicator among many positive indicators that the Soviets are violating the SALT 1 agreements.

The SALT 1 agreement represented the absolute maximum in compromise on the part of the U.S. and absolute minimum by the USSR.

Such information is not restricted to private investigations. In the *Los Angeles Times* of August 8, 1976, Paul Lewis reported concerning a Library of Congress study that, "The Communist forces of the Warsaw Pact outnumber NATO forces in Central and Northern Europe—by more than 2 to 1 in tanks, 5 to 4 in tactical aircraft, and 4 to 3 in troops." He went on to say, "In addition to this numerical edge, the Warsaw Pact enjoys another less obvious advantage; its armies all use the same weapons chiefly of Soviet design, though manufactured throughout the alliance. As a result, Czechoslovakian shells fit Hungarian guns and Polish tanks can pick up spare parts at a Russian depot."

This, of course, gives the Communists very great maneuverability, and drastically reduces supply problems. They save duplication in production, with a consequently huge economic advantage in this area.

Lewis goes on to say, "In contrast, NATO forces look like a military Tower of Babel. Not only are they thinner on the ground, but they also use a bewildering array of different weapons and munitions. Guns, tanks, trucks, jeeps, ammunition, planes, even fuel—all tend to vary according to the nationality of the force in question."

HUGE WASTES BY DUPLICATION

Lewis further quotes the report by Thomas A. Callaghan, Jr., to the effect that NATO was wasting about $10 billion of its annual $40 billion budget for development and production of new weapons, on duplications and inefficient production.

Clearly, standardization is essential, but no one Western power can decide that. With nuclear power virtually equal between U.S.A. and U.S.S.R., the role of conventional weapons is being seen as increasingly important. This area of nonuniformity of weapons is yet another where the Communist forces have a decided advantage. They do not have to deal with competing companies or even countries. They have eliminated that problem years ago!

Philosophically, the West is at a very great disadvantage in all this, and that was seen very clearly in the Vietnam war. One Green Beret Captain put it to one of us (Wilson) like this:

> We can't win. We can't chain our tank drivers to their tanks. We can't shoot them if they refuse to obey an order that is sure to lead to their death.

His meaning was clear. The enemy *will* shoot them for disobedience. Better for that enemy tank driver to have another half-hour of life in a tank with some slight possibility behond that, than certain death for refusing to go into the battle.

Go back to the horrors of World War II. In those years we did terrible things—and we did in Vietnam, with firebombs and all the rest of it. None of it should be condoned, and it is not, except to say that modern war will necessarily be frightening, by the very nature of the weapons available in our state of "advanced" technology.

Nevertheless there is still an essential difference, stemming from our philosophy. We did not keep human prisoners in cages, nor did we withhold necessary medical

attention. To some limited extent even in war we demonstrated basic humanitarianism that stemmed from a
Christian teaching of integrity and even fair play. Limited?—Yes. Expedient?—Yes. Sometimes hypocritical?—
Yes. All that and much more is all too true, but yet our
Western philosophy is essentially different in basis from
materialistic and atheistic Communism. In the so-called
democratic West, a treaty is not merely a piece of paper
to be thrown aside as soon as it is expedient to do so. It is
an agreement that is meant to be honored.

Others in opposition to our philosophy have an entirely
different approach. One result is the necessary buildup of
our own arms and weaponry in a way that is bewildering
and is also stupid—but is yet entirely necessary.

Footnotes: Chapter 5

1. In *Armed Forces Journal International,* April, 1976.
2. *Armed Forces Journal International,* July, 1975.
3. *Ibid.,* p. 33.

Chapter 6

"CONVENTIONAL" WEAPONS AND TAKEOVER BIDS

The threat of war is not limited to nuclear weapons, but so-called "conventional" weapons also offer a great threat. Such weapons are "conventional" only when put alongside the horrific potential of nuclear weapons. Conventional warfare is very much a threat, perhaps even more than nuclear warfare, at least insofar as it relates to the present major powers of the world.

We live in a nuclear age, and we tend now to think in terms only of atomic weapons. This actually is short-sighted, for there are very real dangers associated with "conventional war." This was clearly demonstrated in Vietnam and other military activities around the world.

In one sense it might seem inconceivable that one side would surrender the issue without using the most deadly weapons in its power. However, second thoughts lead to the realization that it would be initiating a self-destruction, a military suicide of far greater loss-potential than anything that could be gained by what some would regard as a relatively small prize, such as a Vietnam victory.

Conventional wars are still likely to be fought in days ahead, and it could be in this very area that the United States will be forced to its knees, a sitting duck as it were for invasion and takeover, without a single atomic weapon being brought into play. It is entirely conceivable that, so long as the invaders did not themselves use atomic weapons, the defenders also would desist. Many American leaders would insist that it would be a responsible judgment to accept defeat rather than to hand the world over to a nuclear holocaust.

It is reasonable to ask, then, "Can this country be sure of successful self-defense in the event of attack?" The answer is a perhaps surprising, "No." We are able to give such an answer because of the information that is available to all who look for it.

THE RELEASE OF
SENSITIVE INFORMATION

We are in an unprecedented age so far as the release of sensitive information is concerned. Much that would surely have been classified as "Top Secret" a decade ago is now public property. In this category is a report in the *Los Angeles Times* of November 25, 1977. Two Associated Press personnel (Special Correspondent Peter Arnett and military writer Fred S. Hoffman) spent months investigating the military potential of the United States to withstand a conventional war. Their findings were staggering and highly disturbing.

They write:

America's ability to fight a major conventional land, air, and sea war has been seriously weakened by shortages in key weapons and ammunition and by other critical deficiences.

The Pentagon has started corrective actions, but it will take from two to six years to cure most of the major shortcomings, according to a two-month investigation by The Associated Press.

The report goes on:

> "Stated frankly and simply, our Army is out-gunned and inadequately equipped," is the way one Army official put it.

> "We have had to live with underequipped tactical fighter units, short falls in airlife capability, an austere . . . air defense force . . . and persistent shortages of aircraft spare parts and some types of munitions," said Gen. David Jones, Air Force Chief of Staff.

> "It will take at least five or six years of concerted effort before the material condition of the entire fleet attains a sustainable satisfactory level," said a Defense Department spokesman describing the Navy.

On the other hand (the report tells us), the Russians have had five years of intensive modernizations. It seems entirely possible that they have developed sufficient hard-hitting and fast-moving ground and air power to attack America's allies in Western Europe, with virtually no warning. The Russians have tank superiority of three to one in the Central European sector; the Allied Air Force has only half the advanced air-to-air missiles it would need in combat with Soviet planes for air supremacy and only half of its required long-range transport planes to bring supplies from the U.S. Warships are seriously handicapped by shortages of parts, with cannibalizing of parts common-place—it is better to have one plane flying, and one ship sailing, than to have four grounded, with each requiring a different part. In the Air Force, the cannibalization rate has doubled in the past three years.

MILITARY FORCES NUMERICALLY WEAK AND STOCKPILES LOW

There are 2.1 million Americans in the military services, this being the smallest number since the Korea War of 1950, while the Navy is down to 468 ships. Hundreds of older ships have been put aside for economy reasons.

On the positive side is the important fact that present military personnel are volunteers, believing in their chosen work. It is also true that planes and other equipment in Europe could be quickly replenished from the United States. It is doubtful, however, if this could be achieved in the vital first 30 days after an attack.

A program has been set in hand to strengthen the fighting machine in Europe over the next several years, and that is pleasant sounding. However, at present (the report declares), "The European war reserves stocks include only about 25% of the tanks required, about one-third of the ammunition, no armored personnel carriers, and no long-barreled, self-propelled artillery, which division commanders say is vital to match the longer ranges of the Soviet field guns."

The same paper, same date, carried another A.P. report headed, "1981-82 Regarded as Critical Time for Western Europe Defense." The subheading was, "U.S. Generals Expect Soviet Union to Finish Equipping Its Forces With Newest Weapons Before That Period." The report stated that:

U.S. generals have circled these dates in their plans for defending Western Europe against a possible massive Soviet ground-air attack.

That is when they expect Russia to finish re-equipping its Army divisions and Air Force squadrons with powerful new weapons and warplanes.

"What do they intend to do with all that new weaponry?" a senior American general reflected recently. "We don't know. But we'd better be ready."

"We'd better be ready." The report indicates that 1979-80 is the target date for recovery in various shortages and inadequacies—a list that is frightening. "We'd better be ready."

It is entirely conceivable that a "conventional" war would suit the Russians very well. Takeover bids from within are not out of the question either. Why fight if you can win by political maneuvering? But that is another topic.

SCAREMONGERS OR REALISTS?

Is all this talk about "conventional" wars and takeover bids to be taken seriously? The words "scaremongers or realists" put the case very well. Some will argue that a book such as this is just another to be added to the list of those already written by the prophets of doom. Perhaps it is, but there is good reason to believe that the Western world is hiding its head in the sand, whereas realism demands a facing of the facts.

Listen to this, from that same *Los Angeles Times* report of November 25, 1977: "The strengthening of Russia's tactical air force and its conversion from a largely defensive to an offensive ground attack role has sharply increased concern about the vulnerability of U.S. air bases, radar stations, supply depots, and command centers."

Why should the Russians change over from defensive to offensive planning? They know that neither they nor anybody else can win in atomic warfare. They *can* win in a conventional war, not by one massive blow that would bring the world to its feet, but by an adaptation of the old domino game, tied in with another favorite of a previous generation, the old-fashioned checkers. Keep moving ahead, removing the pieces of the opposition just one at a time, but eventually making your own pieces kings that can be moved in any direction and can effectively resist any "uncrowned" opposition.

The West still has some "crowns," and still has "uncrowned" pieces as well, but time is running out. While we of the West have thought mainly of atomic bombs and the terror of a nuclear holocaust, the "opposition" has realized the tremendous potential still available with so-called conventional weapons.

The American President can have his little black box, and he will probably never need to go beyond the last state of alert. There will in fact surely be diversions to keep his finger near that button, ensuring that his mind is kept off other seemingly less important strategic matters. These latter, one by one, are likely to bring the United States to the point where ultimately they have no more conventional weapons to send to the Vietnams, the Israels, and the Germanys of the world. What then? And how soon?

There are some aspects about "conventional warfare" that could give us a breathing space—time to recover our sanity and to mend the broken bridges before it is forever too late.

Take the Russian Navy. Because it is more likely to be offensive at the present time than the Navy of any other superpower, it is comforting to take the matter to one further logical point. The Russian Navy cannot safely bring all its forces to one focal point without neglecting other sensitive areas. Raymond Blackman, writing in *The Defense Attache* No. 3 of 1976, puts it this way:

> Whatever may be speculated about the intended purpose of the massive and still growing strength of the Soviet Navy it has to be admitted that this colossal maritime force must of necessity be divided into four separate fleets—in the Far North, the Pacific, the Black Sea and the Baltic—and therefore cannot be approved en masse at much more than a quarter of its strength in any one place at any one time.

We should not on that account consider the danger to be insignificant. We cannot overlook the fact that the fleet is not necessarily required for a period in the Far North, the Black Sea, or the Baltic. What is to prevent a short-time concentration in the Pacific? It is no secret that San Diego harbor is full of ships in mothballs—they are there for everyone taking the ferry ride to see. The same can be said of other areas to the north, stretching up the West Coast of the United States, on the Pacific Seashore. How many units of the Russian Fleet would it take to block those harbors? What demands would be acceded to if a fleet was not-so-gently maneuvering at the several doorways to America, on that vulnerable West Coast? And that is not all.

Weapons stockpiles have fallen to dangerous levels, for various reasons. One is that they were "borrowed" at the time of the 1973 Middle East War, to replace the battle losses of the Israelis. Another is that the German government requested that ammunition be removed to remote depots away from population centers. A related problem—dense population and dense air traffic also—means that training is restricted. Typical is the plight of Army tank units: they are able to shoot only during three periods a year. Both those reasons highlight the constant embarrassment of a government being aware of an opposing buildup that is frightening in its potential.

Then, too, divisions of the Allies into political arenas seriously limit military decisions. The American Command cannot (for example) comfort Israel with the certain assurance that they will have the support they urgently need: the powers that be are all to aware that at some points the Israeli government has policies and practices that Americans as a nation do not endorse.

DEMOCRACY HAS SOME WEAKNESSES

The problem of reconciling racial, political, and humanitarian differences with hard-core military facts is extremely difficult. Changes of government and of leadership take place in the relevant countries, in a way not known by the Russians. They are able to set their sights and to have long-range objectives, as we saw earlier, without the need of counting the votes of the electorate.

No doubt they laugh cynically at the ways our democratic hands are tied by voters whom they in their circumstances can afford to ignore, or to put down in one way or another. They can even influence *our* voters, simply by providing timely funds—and even personnel—paid for by moneys still owed to this country. The takeover bids are serious business. Yet it would be comical if it were not so deadly dangerous. Whoever heard of using a country's own funds to openly undermine it?

Nor do they spend a great deal of their time in their own country either defending their actions, or in arguing about security decisions that ought not to be blazoned on every newspaper, or in appealing to the electorate for the next election when only halfway through the present term of office. Democracy is a wonderful system, and its basic tenets are not surpassed anywhere, but implicit in it are seeds of serious problems and even of ridiculous limitations and frustrations on its leaders.

We have seen another of democracy's problems in relation to the request of the German government to remove stock piles away from densely populated areas. The necessary compliance by U.S. leaders with such requests again points to the basic problems of trying to coordinate separate democratic powers.

THE POWER OF A RABBLE-ROWSER— AROUND THE WORLD

The problem of coordination (or lack of it) exists in all democracies. For example, it takes only one effective rabble-rowser in our democratic system to stir up opposition in a way that is frightening. Behind fronts such as environmental protection and ecology, restrictions are placed that are almost incredible.

One of these authors (Wilson) comes from Australia. In some ways that country's basic philosophy and approach to life is nearer to that of the United States than to any other country, and it too is plagued by extremes of "democracy". Aggressive troublemakers are given great latitude, and the loopholes of the law are constantly exploited to ensure constant harassment to "the establishment." This is especially true in relation to various areas where progress and development should be permitted as a matter or urgency.

In Australia, the unions have become increasingly militant, and in some unions Communists are openly dictating policy. Strikes are called on trivial matters, and the workers themselves are often the ones who suffer most. The "silent majority" appear to reject the policies of the militant union leaders, as witnessed by the December, 1977, sweeping victory of the Liberal (i.e. Conservative) Government led by Malcolm Fraser, but he has his hands full. The unions may not win Government through the Labor (Socialist) Party, but because they are vociferous they can stir up a great deal of support for marches, pickets, and mass rallies which are sometimes frightening in their potential for violence and open lawlessness.

The Australian scene illustrates another "democratic" problem faced by the U.S. in its world-ranging military role. As in other countries, there are strong voices raised (and not only by the unions) against the American presence in Australia. What were accepted a decade ago, perhaps naively, as being weather testing stations are now openly declared as being satellite watching stations, with who knows what weaponry ready to be launched from Australian soil. The "dead heart" (Australia's huge central desert) is suddenly a danger spot of fearful reality, and strong voices are raised in protest.

There are those who believe (or profess to believe, which is a very different matter) that it is the Americans who are the warmongers, that it was the U.S. who intruded into Vietnam when they should have let the Asians work out their own problems. So, the argument goes, they are again intruding, this time onto Australian soil under the guise of peaceful activities such as setting up weather stations.

Not all accept such reasoning. The events of Vietnam, Thailand, Cambodia, and the Philippines are frighteningly and increasingly close to the Australian mainland, and many thinking people are all too aware that Australia simply could not adequately defend its huge area with the lamentably small number of ships, planes, and military equipment at its disposal. The 1977 overwhelming return of the Fraser government, despite near-scandals close to its own ranks, is one indication that the vociferous unions do not fool all of the people all of the time.

THE GIANTS HAVE THEIR HANDS TIED

Nevertheless, the unions' right to free speech is exercised very greatly, and governments conscious of ever-coming elections must pay some attention. This is true in other places beside Australia, as we saw above with the German demands that weaponry be moved away from densely populated areas. Those are the very areas that would need those weapons in the event of attack, but even military leaders must comply when political leaders give them specific instructions.

Military leaders in the U.S. might be amazed at the blindness and even stupidity of some of those who give such instructions, but that is beside the point. Those military leaders are like giants with their hands manacled. They can but obey. They know that blatant takeover bids are proceeding before their eyes, but they are virtually powerless. They can protest, they can raise their voices. But not too loudly, for the boat must not be rocked.

In a coming day those who bound their hands might regret it and wish that the Samson in their midst could destroy the common enemy. Instead they might find that their modern Samson will still destroy the enemy, but in doing so might again be forced to pull down their own house also, destroying all those in it, friend and foe alike. Coming events are casting their ominous shadows.

Chapter 7

ANOTHER GIANT REARS ITS HEAD

We have likened the United States military leaders to the giant Samson, blind, with his eyes out, full of power but having his hands manacled. Russia has been likened to the giant bear it has adopted as its symbol. Its claws are sharp, its appetite for expansion is strong, and it has already emerged from its winter of hibernation.

However, there is another giant also emerging, and its symbol is an ancient one: the dragon. That superpower of Red China might destroy all opposition, and yet it might also be the means of the world's continuation, if only for a short time. If it is not restrained, by the end of the Decade of Shock it too will have come to the point of making takeover demands that must be and will be taken seriously.

THE THREAT FROM THE CHINESE NAVY

The emergence of this great power means that the threat is not only from nuclear warfare and not only from a "conventional" war with Russia. We tend to think of China as the sleeping dragon, and when we allow our unwilling minds to pay any attention to the danger in that quarter, we think of rather "primitive" atomic bombs. Then we go back to sleep: "They've split the atom, but they're way behind us. Maybe in ten years they'll catch up—but not yet."

Out go the lights and soon we are again blissfully unaware that the dragon is stirring. Then comes a newspaper report that changes have taken place—the Chairman has died, "the gang of four" have been exposed, another revolution is taking place. We stir slightly and realize again that sophisticated thinking will bring changes, that technology will improve. Yes, it's a threat. But not to be taken too seriously yet. Anyway, we soothe ourselves; they and the Russians will fight it out—destroy each other you know. And soon we are snoring again.

However, it is not as simple as that. Take one startling fact about the "gang of four." Whoever could have believed that Stalin would have been posthumously "criminalized" so soon after his death?

The point we are making is that even in nondemocratic countries, without people-elected governments, dramatic changes in leadership and in policies take place. As a matter of expediency it is entirely feasible that next year, or the year after, the Russians and the Chinese could be each other's staunchest ally, at least for the time being. If together they could put down all opposition, it then would be a matter of conjecture as to which of the last two would then eliminate the other. Perhaps the Christian teaching about the return of Christ might then be seen as factual after all. It certainly would be an urgent necessity if such a chain of "eliminating events" actually happened, as it very well could.

Let us face this fact. The Chinese dragon is NOT sleeping. Red China has a vast navy—in fact, it is really a series of separate, self-contained navies. There is the North Sea Fleet, the East Sea Fleet, and the South Sea Fleet, and these not only mean that China itself is a great bastion, very well protected, but it is able to offer a threat as a springboard against any aggressors from any area. The January 18, 1978, *Los Angeles Times* reported on Senator Alan Cranston's recent visit to China. He stated that he was discouraged by the Peking government's "acceptance of the absolute inevitability of world war.''

SUBMARINES ALL NUCLEAR—"BY THE END OF THE DECADE"?

The Red China Navy is third only to U.S.A. and Russia in submarine strength, some being armed with ballistic missile launchers, but conventionally powered, while others are nuclear powered but conventionally armed, utilizing torpedo tubes.

Commenting on this, Raymond Blackman writes in *The Defense Attache*[1] mentioned above, "This foreshadows the building of a nuclear powered and ballistic missile armed submarine at the indigenous shipyard by the end of the decade.''

Notice those words, ''the end of the decade.'' Blackman is referring to *this* decade, the 1970's, not the 1980's. We are not presenting science fiction, but fact. The Red Chinese Navy has over 1900 vessels. Blackman further tells us:

> A rather startling feature of the recent Chinese naval resurgence is the number of fast attack craft (motor patrol vessel and MTB type) built or acquired over the past few years. These run into 725 craft, comprising 115 guided missile vessels, 460 gunboats, and 250 torpedo boats, and they constitute the largest fleet of fast attack craft in the world. One ponders their objective, if not largely defensive.

That is not all. The Red Chinese have 500 aircraft, and their new construction programs include warships fitted with flight decks and aircraft hangars. They have a vast population reservoir (over 800 million) on which to draw, and by known standards their potential is virtually unlimited. As Blackman says, ''The Chinese Navy of the immediate future could upset the whole balance of sea power East of Suez, and require the navies of the Soviet and American superpowers to revise and escalate their forward procurement and deployment.''

Who pays the price of providing for self-defense? You and I, at *this* time. Who pays if we don't pay now? You and I, but also our children and our grandchildren. That is, of course, if the world survives. Such a statement is taken seriously today as we approach the coming Decade.

Footnotes: Chapter 7

1. Raymond Blackman, in *The Defense Attache,* No. 3, (1976).

Chapter 8

MILITARY ARMS PROLIFERATION

We have written at length about the preparations being undertaken by the United States, and we have seen that there has been an alarming loss of supremacy. We have recognized that Russia has fast moved towards equality with the U.S., and in some ways has gone beyond this great country. We have briefly considered the role of Red China and recognize that the sleeping dragon is no longer sleeping after all.

However, the problem does not end there, for it is no longer possible to think of the means of international destruction being only in the hands of the superpowers. Times have changed. In World War II the big four were United States, Great Britain, Russia, and France. It would be quite unrealistic today to ignore other great powers such as Red China, Japan, West Germany—but even then the counting does not stop. The dreadful and terrifying fact is that there is an increasing number of nations around the world who have access to nuclear power. As Bernard T. Feld says, "The number of opportunities for nuclear conflict . . . increases in geometric proportion to the number of nations possessing nuclear bombs."

We shall see that other nations besides the superpowers

now have access to terror weapons, but first let us consider some other background material.

THE EQUIVALENT OF 1,300,000
HIROSHIMA ATOMIC BOMBS

According to a recent U.N. report on the arms race the combined explosive power of the 12,000 strategic nuclear warheads in the U.S. and Russia is the equivalent of 1,300,000 Hiroshima atomic bombs. In addition, there are about 48,000 smaller tactical nuclear weapons with the equivalent power of another 50,000 Hiroshima A-Bombs. The arms race costs at least $350 billion a year, and since World War II direct costs of the race have passed the $6,000,000,000,000 mark. (In 1976 the world military expenditure was over $400 billion.)[1]

According to the September 6, 1976 *Newsweek* Rear Admiral Gene R. Larocque, head of the Center for Defense Information, stated the U.S. has sold or given away more than 18,000 missiles, ships, and aircraft capable of carrying nuclear weapons. He says, "It is now within the capacity of almost every nation to develop or obtain nuclear weapons to go with those missiles, ships, and aircraft." He notes the U.S. is pursuing an, "Uncontrolled, unplanned, hectic effort—to sell weapons all over the world to any country which can afford them . . . ," and that this "will reduce national security in the long run." It is widely believed—rightly or wrongly—that part of the reason for these sales is to help offset our massive oil bill which is causing serious balance of payments problems.

Frank Barnaby, Director of the prestigious Stockholm International Peace Research Institute, states: "The arms trade is now virtually out of control."[2]

When we look at the world as a whole for the period 1955 to 1975, the international trade of major weapons increased 500%.[3] Yet in 1974 international peacekeeping outlays amounted to considerably less than one percent of military expenditures.[4] Half the world's school age children are not in schools, one-third of all adults are illiterate, and nations spend far more on military forces than health care.[5] Forty to fifty percent of the world's best qualified scientists and engineers (about 400,000) devote themselves to the field of military research and development.[6] It is a startling fact that 60% of U.S. and Soviet satellites are military in purpose, the U.S. having spent some $30 billion on military space activities.[7]

The world stands "between a rock and a hard place." With the OPEC oil-cartel of 1973, oil prices quadrupled, international debt soared, and, all of a sudden, energy was the number one issue. The vital importance of energy can hardly be understated, nor can the overreliance of most countries on "cheap energy" be ignored. Hence the Arab price hike contributed directly to nuclear proliferation.

Countries who could once meet their energy bills on "cheap oil" now are prepared to believe that if they are to have energy independence, the ultimate solution must be nuclear. The argument is that despite potential hazards, nuclear power is far less dangerous than the possibilities envisioned by not going nuclear, especially energy dependence that may lead to political submission to another country. Economic breakdown could result from a country's inability to pay for oil, with resulting social chaos and other serious problems.

There is also the belief—which we shall challenge—that the world will run out of oil by about the year 2,000 anyway, and so there is a lineup to join the nuclear club. A main problem is that once a country decides to "go nuclear" for energy, it inherits at the same time the possibility of "going nuclear" with bombs.

NUCLEAR PROLIFERATION SINCE 1945

The following outline shows nuclear proliferation since 1945:

Country With Nuclear Bombs	Year Occurred
U.S.	1945
U.S.S.R.	1949

Britain	1952
France	1960
China	1964
India	1974
Israel	1975?

Many countries are seeking to join the nuclear club: Turkey openly discusses its developing of nuclear weapons and Libya's President Qaddafi has said, "We will have our share of these new weapons." South Africa has threatened to build one. Pakistan's Prime Minister warned India that if there is further atomic bomb development by them, "We will eat leaves and grass, even go hungry, but we will have to get one of our own." The Shah of Iran has said, "If every upstart [country] in the [Arab] region acquires atomic bombs, then Iran must have them as well." Other Arab countries, particularly in the face of Israel having the bomb, are exploring means of obtaining it also.[8]

According to Harvard's Daniel Yergin, author of *Shattered Peace,* present plans allow for 40 countries to have nuclear energy programs by 1985, and most of them have enough raw material to make over 30 bombs each. By 1990, reactors in the Third World *alone* will be able to produce enough material for 3,000 nuclear bombs a year—a disturbing fact when we consider how international terrorism is on the increase. By 1995 as many as 100 nations could have the capacity for nuclear bombs.[9]

An informal poll of 21 leading U.S. nonproliferation experts, at a private meeting in March, 1975, indicated that 18 expected anywhere from 1 to 14 more countries to develop the bomb by 1985. None expected the line to be held at six.[10] The inequalities, loopholes, and the inadequacy of the Nuclear Nonproliferation Treaty (NPT) has caused dozens of nations to consider entry into the nuclear club, particularly in politically volatile Asia. As a result of the (Vietnam induced) decline of U.S. credibility as a stabilizing power in the region (this being the most crucial factor in the proliferation scene), the balance of power in Asia will be increasingly more complex and less stable than in Europe.[11] There are open fears of inevitable "small nation atomic wars" which invariably would draw in the large superpowers.[12] China has even publicly urged Asian nuclear proliferation.[13]

Nonnuclear countries cannot be expected to refrain from "going nuclear" when the nuclear powers have shown no progress in arms control themselves. Particularly as a result of the energy crises, nuclear power is seen as more and more desirable, and over 50 nations have refused to ratify the Nuclear Nonproliferation Treaty. In September, 1977, at the annual conference of the 110-nation International Atomic Energy Agency, most nations made it clear they would continue with plans for fast-breeder reactors and nuclear reprocessing.[14]

Actually there is considerable incentive for countries to go nuclear. They have everything to gain—power, prestige, energy—and it can be seriously argued that they have little to lose. They are part of a world where power means security, a world in which the superpowers having nuclear weapons break commitments about limiting arms escalation.

The May, 1975, Review Conference of the Parties to the Nonproliferation Treaty, initially called "The most important arms control conference since World War II." was a dismal failure.[15] Then in 1976 Bernard T. Feld, M.I.T. Professor of Physics and Director of *The Bulletin of The Atomic Scientists,* stated that during that year, "on the whole, there have been more steps backwards than ahead . . . we have moved appreciably closer to the brink in a number of respects, but we are still short of the abyss . . . ."[16]

CHEAPER NUCLEAR BOMBS

A factor greatly increasing the chances of proliferation is "laser isotope separation." A new way to produce materials for nuclear bombs has been developed, and it is far easier and cheaper than the previous method. Laser enrichment plants are expected to be in commercial operation within six years.[17] The process uses lasers to separate the isotopes of uranium, and one of the scientists working on the project stated in 1977, "The whole world had better be a little bit uneasy, because it will be a whole lot easier to make bombs."[18]

There is also the possibility of nuclear countries bargaining with nonnuclear countries in "exchange deals." Would India share its nuclear know-how with Arab countries in exchange for desperately needed oil concessions? If "the price is right," will a nuclear country sell its technology for purely financial gain? The ominous possibilities are upon us.

Countries do not buy conventional weapons with the intent of using them immediately (unless there is war): they buy them *in case they are needed*, and especially in case it becomes necessary to insure their own survival. One of the most obvious conclusions that can be drawn from the lack of nuclear arms control, and the increase in proliferation, is that countries *assume* the need for such weapons. In a world where there are multiple threats to survival, such as from energy crises, famines, and terrorism, and where countries are dependent on others for their life's blood (oil), to have nuclear weapons is one of the few factors that can produce a feeling of security. The fact of having nuclear weapons can be used to force what the country feels is justice toward itself. If it cannot get that, by having an atomic "backup" it knows it can deliver retribution.

It is simply not human nature to lie down and die. Multiple crises are involved, and there is always the prospect of human inefficiency and numerous uncertainties. Too many decisions must be made too fast, and, as a result, issues relating to nationality, humanitarianism, and thought for consequences become significantly clouded, with rational judgment affected. In times of emergency, "normal things" are offside, and quickly.

THE NEW NUCLEAR PRESTIGE

There are numerous other reasons why it is advantageous for countries to go nuclear. One is the prestige and influence developed almost overnight. For example, an Argentine legislator who recently introduced a bill calling on the Government to develop the bomb stated: "Recent events have demonstrated that nations gain increasing recognition in the international arena in accordance with their power." He cited China as an example: she was purposely ignored by the great powers until she went nuclear.[19]

We have already referred to the Israelis, and we again ask ourselves what three million Israelis would do, facing a hostile Arab world of well over 100 million? One can easily imagine them being pushed to the wall. And, after their experiences under Hitler, they are not about to lose the only homeland they have had in 2,000 years.

What will a "have-not" country do, when, sensing a desperate future, it realized that with a nuclear bomb there is the hope of food for its people by the expedient of nuclear blackmail? Nuclear weapons provide the edge over any potential aggressor States. As more noncommunist States realize that the U.S. cannot be relied upon to protect them in every circumstance, and that indeed in the future the U.S. will have enough troubles of its own, the tendency to go nuclear for that country's own safety is likely to become a dominating concern. A natural consequence will be that as more and more nations go nuclear, other nations will feel even greater insecurity. It begins to look as if only a world dictator can solve the complex issues of world peace.

REASONS FOR INCREASED CHANCES
OF NUCLEAR WAR

Obviously nuclear proliferation significantly increases the chances of nuclear war. More countries having atomic bombs means that a larger number of people have at their disposal the means to start a nuclear war. The chances that political instability, terrorism, and/or conventional war will result in the use of "the bomb" increases when more parties involved have the potential to use it.

In an editorial of the *Bulletin of the Atomic Scientists* (September, 1975), Samuel H. Day reminds us that the world stands literally at the brink of an irreversible pro-liferation of nuclear war-making potential. He reminds us of the dreadful fact that millions will live or die depending on calculations and miscalculations, whims and passions of not just one person, but of a growing number of people who have the capacity to inflict immediate and almost unimaginable destruction on other peoples. Day reminds us that the situation is so much more dangerous today than it was 30 years ago because it is no longer a slow drift towards nuclear catastrophe, but is in fact now a headlong rush. In an earlier editorial of the same journal (January, 1975) he pointed out that some two dozen nations are fast approaching a capability in nuclear weaponry, with every indication that many of them intend to achieve that capacity; as a result the risk of sudden nuclear holocaust is being heightened immeasurably.

The prospect is frightening. It is more than that—it is terrifying. In the Bible, at Revelation, Chapter 6 we read of the stars of the heavens falling unto the earth and mountains and islands being moved out of their places. We learn of kings and great men, the rich and the chief captains and other mighty men, as well as slaves and those who are free, hiding themselves in the dens and the rocks of the mountains and saying to the mountains and the rocks, "Fall on us, and hide us from the face of Him Who sits on the throne, and from the wrath of the Lamb. For the great day of His wrath is come, and who shall be able to stand?" (Rev. 6:13-17).

It is certainly not hard to see the possibility of those verses being fulfilled in the near future.

Footnotes: Chapter 8

1. Frank Barnaby, "The Mounting Prospect of Nuclear War," *Bulletin of the Atomic Scientists,* June, 1977, p. 15; *Los Angeles Times,* Oct. 16, 1977.
2. Frank Barnaby, "World Armament and Disarmament," *Bulletin of the Atomic Scientists,* June, 1976, p. 26.
3. *Ceres,* May-June, 1976, p. 14.
4. "The Militarization Of The Global Economy," *World Issues,* February-March, 1977, p. 26.
5. *Ibid.,* p. 25.
6. Frank Barnaby, "World Armament And Disarmament," *Bulletin of the Atomic Scientists,* June, 1976, p. 26.
7. Frank Barnaby, "The Mounting Prospect Of Nuclear War," *Bulletin of the Atomic Scientists,* June, 1976, p. 17.
8. Daniel Yergin, "The Terrifying Prospect: Atomic Bombs Everywhere," *Atlantic Monthly,* April, 1977, p. 47; *U.S. News and World Report,* May 12, 1975, p. 68; *Orbis,* Fall, 1975, p. 934.
9. *Ibid.,* p. 47
10. Lincoln P. Bloomfield, "Nuclear Spread and World Order," *Foreign Affairs,* July, 1975, p. 743.
11. Dougherty, "Nuclear Proliferation In Asia," *Orbis,* Fall, 1975, especially pp. 949-57.
12. Robert S. Elgant, "Spur To Nuclear Race Seen in Viet Fall," *Los Angeles Times,* May 25, 1975.
13. *Ibid.*
14. Don Cook, "Few Nations Stop Nuclear Planning," *L.A. Times,* October 2, 1977.
15. William Epstein, "Failure At The NPT Review Conference," *Bulletin of the Atomic Scientists,* September, 1975, pp. 46-48.
16. Bernard T. Feld, "1967-1977 Time For A Shock," *Bulletin of the Atomic Scientists,* January, 1977, p. 8.

17. Barry M. Casper, "Laser Enrichment: A New Path To Proliferation?", *Bulletin of the Atomic Scientists,* January, 1977, pp. 28-29.
18. *Ibid.,* p. 28.
19. Lincoln Bloomfield, "Nuclear Spread and World Order," *Foreign Affairs,* July, 1975, p. 747.

Chapter 9

A TREND THAT CANNOT BE REVERSED

Proliferation such as that elaborated in our previous chapter means that both the U.S. and the U.S.S.R. might well lose control over their own destinies. Every new outbreak of war will carry a greater risk of nuclear war, particularly if and when mineral resources, energy, and food get scarcer, as climate worsens, as the East-West political tensions harden, and as the world's North-South economic strains increase.

WE ARE ENTERING THE SECOND NUCLEAR AGE

Harvard's Daniel Yergin questions whether or not it is already too late to remedy matters. He puts the situation tersely, yet very clearly, by a simple illustration:

> In an automobile accident there is the long moment before impact, when you see the other vehicle coming toward you, and you realize that a collision is imminent, and yet you cannot believe that it is going to happen. At last, you hear the sound of colliding metal, and you know that it too late.

The people of the world are at such a moment, on course for a nuclear collision. The question is whether it is already too late to change direction. Nuclear warfare has been a possibility for more than three decades. But suddenly the threat has intensified, not because of political instability, but simply because of the prospect of widespread proliferation of nuclear armament. It is not too much to say that we are entering the second Nuclear Age—the age of proliferation.[1]

There is the question—"Is it too late to change direction?" The frightening probability is that the trend cannot be reversed.

Another problem area is that of nuclear weapons accidents. Few people realize how frequently they occur and just how fortunate we have been so far. The authoritative Stockholm International Peace Research Institute Yearbook (1977) states there have been at least 125 such accidents in the last 30 years—one every three months.[2]

PUBLIC APATHY IS NOT
REALLY THE PROBLEM

Many authorities feel that public apathy has much to do with the accelerating arms race. Samuel Day states, "It constitutes perhaps the most ominous of the various forces pulling the world toward a nuclear holocaust."[3]

There are several reasons for this:

1. Underground testing removes visible signs of the danger.
2. A hope (admittedly false) in the SALT agreements.
3. Inability of the human mind to comprehend the magnitude and implications of what is involved in all-out nuclear war.
4. The nonuse of atomic weapons in 30 years.
5. Finally, there is a feeling of powerlessness to really do anything about the situation, especially

when people have enough day-to-day problems to concern them already.

Another factor is not so much apathy, as the feeling we are elaborating—that there *is* no solution to the problem, that the trend cannot be reversed. When powerful countries such as Russia and China openly declare themselves your enemy to the death, what can you do beyond hope your side will be stronger? When these opposing countries are known for not being trustworthy and for using any means (e.g. détente) for justifying their ends (world Communism), then it becomes nearly impossible to trust them and to insure adequate compliance in any treaty.

One very real questions is, how practical and how wise is it to trust your avowed enemies? When Breshnev speaks of "the atrocities of the fascist [U.S.] brutes" . . . and when Russia and China almost daily make vicious ideological attacks on America, in their papers, radios, and television . . . when they teach their children to become "militant, convinced, atheists" and to hate Americans and other "Western Imperialists"—yet are totally oblivious to perhaps as many as 90,000,000 people in their own countries they have murdered—what can be expected? How do you secure peace when the Communists are committed to world dominion?

This is one reason why Professor Emeritus of Psychiatry, Jerome Frank of Johns Hopkins University states: "Given the depth of mutual distrust between the Soviet Union and the United States, the goal of reducing armaments by mutual agreement with verification seems a hopeless goal."[4] He also points out that, as a threat system, deterrence is inherently unstable when both sides get to the point of equal strength—there is no longer a clear advantage that one possesses over the other. Mutual distrust and fear can reach a point of intensity where rational calculation ceases, where the desire to destroy the enemy is greater than the desire to stay alive, or where the benefits of war seem to outweigh the cost.

He also notes:

> Another tension-producing aspect of deterrence
> is that its effectiveness depends on each side's
> ability to convince the other of its determination
> to carry out the threat if necessary. In short, it
> includes a large component of bluff. As Sec-
> retary Henry Kissinger wrote before he was in
> politics: "Deterrence depends above all on psy-
> chological criteria . . . For purposes of deter-
> rence a bluff taken seriously is more useful than
> a serious threat interpreted as a bluff." This state
> of affairs puts a premium on military muscle
> flexing, belligerent statements, and the like.

> In this context, disarmament negotiations have
> virtually no chance of success, because a pro-
> posal that is acceptable to one side is by this very
> fact unacceptable to the other. The true, if un-
> avowed, aim of every nation that goes into a
> disarmament conference is to increase its real or
> relative armament to the detriment of its rivals.
> Thus "disarmament" turns out to be but one of
> the forms the arms race can take.

The Helsinki and Vladivostok accords bear witness to
the fact that Soviet and U.S. leaders are still operating on
this principle.

"Thus, deterrence and disarmament negotiations between relatively equal powers have always failed and have,
eventually, resulted in war."[5] Unfortunately the trends
cannot be reversed by political maneuvering.

ALARMING ARAB ARMS PURCHASE

Another problem is that the Arab world, with vast oil
profits, is buying arms at alarming rates. Much of the oil
profits of $56 billion in 1974 are being used for military
purchases—one country alone bought over $7.5 billion
worth of arms from the U.S. during 1974-75.[6]

Frank Barnaby, the Director of SIPRI, notes that from 1973 to 1975 the U.S. received orders for military equipment from OPEC countries to a total value of $13.7 billion. As a result of this, added to the already on-going Arab-Israeli arms race, the Middle East has become the most militarized region in all the world. It is even possible that the Middle Eastern armies are more up-to-date than those of the NATO countries.[7]

WHAT PROSPECT FOR ARMS CONTROL?

The failure of arms control methods is stated no better than by a man who helped develop the atomic bomb and has for half a lifetime done his best to control it. We must understand that if *two* countries cannot agree to halting the arms race, there is virtually no chance for twenty countries to do so.

MIT Professor of Physics, Bernard T. Feld, makes the point that after 30 years of intensive efforts, we are actually behind where we started. He points out that numbers, types, forms, strengths, and all other destructive aspects of nuclear arms have been expanding almost unhindered, despite the fact that the horrors of Hiroshima and Nagasaki seemed to have made the world determined that nuclear weapons would never again be used. Feld makes the point that we appear to be "in grave danger of evaporating from human consciousness" the memory of those horrors. He goes on to say, after half a lifetime in the pursuit of restrictions on nuclear arms, that he is reluctantly but inexorably forced to the conclusion that "the arms control approach simply does not work in today's world—a different approach is essential if nuclear disaster is to be averted."[8]

In October of 1977, Sidney Lens, author of *The Day Before Doomsday,* wrote that:

Since 1945, American and other diplomats have met at least 5,000 times to discuss disarmament and arms control, but not a single warhead has been destroyed as a result of all these meetings . . . The SALT II agreement in principle reached between Leonid Brezhnev and Gerald Ford in December, 1974, allows each side to *double* the number of deliverable warheads and places virtually no limits on improving the quality of existing weapons. The Nonproliferation Treaty, signed in 1968, is riddled with loopholes that enable even its signatories to maintain a standby capacity to assemble nuclear weapons.[9]

ARMS CONTROL AGREEMENTS ALWAYS FAIL

Bernard Feld points out that in the case of *every* important nuclear arms control agreement since 1963 the treaty has resulted in an "arms control disaster," and had not decreased, but *increased*, weapons development. He states, "The results to date of the Strategic Arms Limitation Talks—products of five years of determined bilateral negotiations, of twice as many years of informal and formal technical preparations, and of three summit meetings—add up to a large step backwards . . . [and have] resulted in a more-than tenfold increase in the over-kill capabilities of both sides."[10] He notes that the failure to curb new technological advances in nuclear weaponry has given the go-ahead to military planners on all kinds of new weapons schemes.

He points out that both sides have been moving steadily from the earlier posture of reliance on nuclear weapons as a sole purpose of deterring a first strike by the other side. Now instead they are thinking of postures that can only be interpreted as being preparations for those weapons to be used in any conflict, against any kind of target, no matter what might be the actions of the other side. This is a regrettable departure from the structure so painfully hammered out over 26 post-World War II years, and Feld points out that it "can only lead to unmitigated disaster."[11]

Frank Barnaby concurs: "The fact that these weapons are being developed and deployed without any significant restraint is firm evidence that each of the two great powers is striving for a first strike capability."[12]

With the vast amounts of money being spent on weapons research, the possibility is always present of an impressive technological breakthrough, allowing one side to actually win (or to think it can win) a nuclear war, and suffer minimal damage. One example of the many technological improvements is noted when we compare the first atomic bomb exploded over Hiroshima, with the Minuteman III MIRV. The MIRV is *17 times* more powerful, and yet weighs *40 times less* than the Hiroshima bomb.

Is there any solution? Many argue it is too late, and there is good reason to believe that this assessment is correct—that the situation is far too complex for merely *human* solutions. Apart from a united world state, nuclear proliferation is inevitable. Sidney Lens echoes the feelings of many when he says:

> We must admit there is a long road ahead, and that the bomb dictates immense changes in the way human beings relate to each other, as well as in the concept of the nation state.
>
> The need to establish international mechanisms to deal with proliferation, population, pollution, exploration and exploitation of ocean seabeds, and hunger was stressed by the late U.N. Secretary-General U Thant. None of these problems, he said, could be solved within the narrow framework of the nation state.[13]

As Frank Barnaby states in his article *"The Mounting Prospects of Nuclear War:"* "To say that nuclear disarmament is impossible . . . may be tantamount to saying nuclear war is inevitable."[14]

In late 1977 NATO in essence gave approval for U.S. deployment of the Neutron Bomb on The European Central Front (though recent developments have placed it in a holding pattern).[15] The inherent possibilities are frightening, and it is continually relevant to ask, "Where does it lead to?" Soon we shall know. Perhaps a monster is soon to be born.

Even a spiritual revival as great any the world has known possibly would not be sufficient to reverse the trend, and what other hope for the world is there? The Decade of Shock will tell us in no uncertain terms. Perhaps we are rushing into the arms of a world dictator. Or of a Messiah?

Footnotes: Chapter 9

1. Daniel Yergin, "The Terrifying Prospect: Atomic Bombs Everywhere," *Atlantic Monthly,* April, 1977, p. 47.
2. Frank Barnaby, "The Mounting Prospects Of Nuclear War," *Bulletin of the Atomic Scientists,* June, 1977, p. 15.
3. Editorial, "Our Unfinished Business," *Bulletin of the Atomic Scientists,* December, 1975, p. 9.
4. Jerome D. Frank, M.D., "Psychological Aspects Of The Nuclear Arms Race," *Bulletin of the Atomic Scientists,* April, 1976, p. 24.
5. *Ibid.,* pp. 22-23.
6. R.M. Myers, "Letters," *Bioscience,* April, 1976, p. 236.
7. Frank Barnaby, "World Armament And Disarmament," *Bulletin of the Atomic Scientists,* June, 1976, p. 30.
8. Bernard T. Feld, "Arms Control Or What?" *Bulletin of the Atomic Scientists,* November, 1975, p. 5.
9. Sidney Lens, "The Arms Race: A Primer," *The Progressive,* October, 1977, p. 42.
10. Bernard T. Feld, "The Charade of Piecemeal Arms Limitation," *Bulletin of the Atomic Scientists,* January, 1975, p. 8.

11. *Ibid.*
12. Frank Barnaby, "World Armament And Disarmament," *Bulletin of the Atomic Scientists,* June, 1976, p. 32.
13. Sidney Lens, "The Arms Race: A Primer," *The Progressive,* October, 1977, p. 42.
14. *Bulletin of the Atomic Scientists,* June, 1977, p. 20.
15. Don Cook, "NATO Approval For U.S. Deployment Of Neutron Bomb Expected Early Next Year?", *Los Angeles Times,* December 7, 1977.

Chapter 10

ENERGY

The coming decade will embrace other problems besides those of war and terror from the skies or from other nations. Energy and economics will be two of the keys in The Decade of Shock, the 1980's. Most people believe there is an energy crisis, and that it is serious. If the trillions of dollars spent on arms had been spent on developing solar energy and fusion research, we might not have a serious problem today, but if the facts are as we are urged to believe, it is now too late to avoid yet another shock in the decade we face. The stark reality is that the world has too many problems to generate enough capital to solve our crises. Energy is possibly yet another area of major crisis. We say "possibly" because the whole matter of an energy crisis is challengeable, as we shall see.

We face a whole series of crises. We have said that previous generations have faced one major crisis at a time, and that has been enough to cause war after war. Now we recognize a whole series of interlocking crises, and the net result is that we are being prepared for a takeover by a world dictator. Only a decade ago the then Secretary-General of the U.N. gave the world ten years to put its house in order. In that time the world situation has not improved, but has worsened considerably. In 1969 he stated:

> I do not wish to seem overdramatic, but I can only conclude from the information that is available to me as Secretary-General, that the Members of the United Nations have perhaps ten years left in which to subordinate their ancient quarrels and launch a global partnership to curb the arms race, to improve the human environment, to defuse the population explosion, and to supply the required momentum to development efforts. If such a global partnership is not forged within the next decade, then I very much fear that the problems I have mentioned will have reached such staggering proportions that they will be beyond our capacity to control.[1]

Former Secretary of State Dean Rusk warned in early 1978 that we face "literally lethal issues," and that unless our problems are soon solved, a new general war is nearly inevitable and "the human race will face a catastrophe such as it has never faced before."[1a]

We do not believe the entire world will be destroyed in The Decade of Shock. However, the situation in the economic, political, moral, technological, energy, resource, environment, and food areas will increasingly clear the way for the rise of a world dictator. It is likely that he will be responsible at least indirectly for the death of half the world's population, together with inconceivable environmental destruction.

Outlandish? Inconceivable? The World War II slaughter of Jews—the horrors of some Nazi war camps—the incredible sufferings of some Prisoners of War in the Pacific—the more recent sufferings in some of the African countries such as Uganda—they, too, are incredible. We like to blot out the memories of atrocities against fellow humans—but they still happened. The Decade of Shock will see some things equally incredible.

Let us briefly consider some aspects of the energy crisis as it has been presented before the world.

OIL: BLACK GOLD

From 1975 to 1976, U.S. dependence on Arab oil doubled. In 1977, 50% of all the oil the U.S. used came from abroad, and over $45 billion left the country to pay for it.[2] The sobering reality that these figures highlight is that we are no longer an independent nation. Our ideals, and even our freedom, depend to some extent on the whims of other countries. Our trade deficit has gone from $9.3 billion in 1976 to over $30 billion in 1977, largely because of oil and gas imports.[3] Every one percent increase in the price of oil causes a $400 to $500 million increase in the trade deficit.[4]

At times we read critical arguments that there is plenty of oil in this country, and large areas are nominated where oil has been found and sealed off. No doubt there is much truth in such assertions, but it is also true that it would be an act of total stupidity to use up all the resources available, with nothing whatever to fall back on, both for domestic consumption and for possible military use (at home or abroad). That might be part of the answer as to the sealing off of oil wells.

If there was another oil embargo or price increase of the magnitude of the 1975 economic disaster, there must be some protection. There must obviously be at least a buffer against total economic collapse. Another oil crisis of that magnitude could have such far-reaching effects that the American way of life could be forever dramatically changed, and its effects could be just as drastic in a number of other Western countries. And yet, according to the *Los Angeles Times* of February 8, 1978, even without another oil embargo, oil prices are expected to double to $25 a barrel, or more, by 1985. Deputy Energy Secretary John O'Leary was quoted as saying: "We are walking into a disaster in the next three or four years, with our eyes wide open." The *Times* of March 30, 1978, reported that according to computer models, even at $17 a barrel, in

1983, the U.S. will be paying $102 billion a year for foreign crude alone, up from $45 billion in 1978.

WORLDWIDE RECOGNITION

On June 23-24, 1977, the Ministers of the 25 nation OECD (Organization for Economic Cooperation and Development) met for a council meeting. Six main concerns emerged, among them their recognition of the energy crisis. According to the July, 1977, *OECD Observer,* the Ministers recognized that an imbalance between world energy supply and demand, which could occur as early as the 1980's, would have severe economic, social, and political repercussions in OECD countries and throughout the world. They expressed their determination to avoid that situation by stronger action to conserve energy, and to develop alternative sources of energy, and to include sound energy policies in their overall economic approach.

Despite the warning, little has been done. The U.S. is an OECD member and is supposed to take the lead, but according to Chevron President, D.L. Bower, at the *Time* Energy Conference of 1977, "Up to now our Government's approach to energy problems has been largely characterized by indifference, indecision, and delay."[5] This is inexcusable, but human. One reason for the OECD concern was the 1977 revised estimate that net oil imports in 1985 were expected to be 70% *higher* than thought in 1974.[6] They warned: "We continue to be faced with a very serious energy problem which has major economic implications. Any slackening of efforts to meet even current goals [of conservation and increased production] will only further intensify the gravity of the situation."[7]   .

The balance of payments problems resulting from oil imports was expected to start declining in 1974. The 1977 revised estimates point to a further $20 billion increase between 1977-1980 in the oil bill, indicating continued balance of payments problems.[8]

According to some authorities, the world could start to run out of oil (i.e. production will peak) as early as 1983, and at present, oil supplies the largest part of our energy needs. We have abundant coal, but it is argued that there is not enough time to substitute it for oil—that historically it has taken us 40-50 years to substitute a new energy source so that it could supply just 10% of the nation's needs. Some of the world's leaders think atomic energy will solve the problem, but at present that appears to be a lost cause for several reasons that we haven't the space to discuss. The *Los Angeles Times* of December 18, 1977, outlined some of the problems.

There is also the problem of policy-making machinery in all countries being oriented to the short term, when in fact we are dealing with a long-term problem. A decision made today may take up to 10 years to produce a visible impact. It is generally agreed we must rely on now-operable energy sources such as oil, coal, gas, and nuclear energy for at least three to four decades. Alternate sources cannot be developed fast enough to meet world demand, yet we are warned that we do not have enough energy to get us by for even two decades without massive economic disruption.

IS THERE A CONSPIRACY?

There is another possibility, hinted at throughout this chapter. That is, there is not, and never has been, a true oil crisis except insofar as one was manufactured for political purposes.

It is an open secret that there are massive reserves of oil within the U.S., reserves that have never been fully explained. That is not surprising, for various security reasons. Nor is it totally beyond explanation that new finds in Texas (and elsewhere) should be capped, for they could well be intended as a protection against that expected "rainy day."

Such decision-making is understandable. What is not so understandable is the withholding of information as to the massive quantities of oil available to the U.S. from the findings off Alaska.

Rev. Lindsey Williams, missionary in Alaska, was chaplain to the pipeline at Prudeaux Bay and the surrounding areas for the 2½ years it took for the pipeline to be built.

At a public conference at Glenwood Springs in Colorado in February, 1978, he declared that there is no oil crisis—that the Prudeaux Bay area alone has enough oil to supply the world, even on projected rates of increase, for 200 years. He is producing a book with facts, figures, and names, indicating that there is no oil crisis—and never was.

When pressed for a reason for the apparent manipulation of the general public—with long gas lines when in fact massive supplies were readily available—he claimed that it was an attempt with the ultimate purpose of socializing the great oil cartels.

Such an argument will be immediately rejected by many as unrealistic. On the other hand, socializing of major industries could be part of a superplan leading ultimately to world dictatorship. Time will tell—possibly that time will be during the Decade of Shock.

Footnotes: Chapter 10

1. Meadows, et al, *The Limits To Growth,* (NY: New American Library, Second Ed. 1975), p. 21.
1a. *Los Angeles Times,* Jan. 31, 1978; February 3, 1978.
2. "What In The World?", *Los Angeles Times* Editorial, October 11, 1977.
3. *Los Angeles Times,* November 21, 1977, p. 12, part 1 (see November 7).
4. *Ibid.,* November 7, 1977.
5. "Opening The Debate," *Time,* April 25, 1977, p. 28.
6. "The World Energy Outlook For The Next Ten Years," *The OECD Observer,* March, 1977, p. 4.
7. *Ibid.*
8. *Ibid.*

Chapter 11

CHEMICAL POLLUTION

In the last several years our individual chances of getting cancer have gone from 1 in 8 to 1 in 5, largely as a result of the thousands of poisonous chemicals modern man uses.[1] *Newsweek* recently stated:

> Poisonous chemicals like Kepone, PCB's, PBB's, and Mirex are endangering the health of Americans in a growing number of states. They have been flushed into rivers and lakes, sprayed over crops, and allowed to float through the air. Virtually indestructible, they remain in the tissues of wildlife and humans, and seemingly healthy people may suffer from their toxic effects twenty years after exposure . . . . The highly toxic chemicals have already contaminated waters and cropland in more than a dozen states . . . . Mirex has been sprayed across 200 million acres of farmland in the South.[2]

The *Los Angeles Times* of April 4, 1978, reported that Dr. Irving Selikoff, an authority on poison and cancer-producing agents said that polybrominated biphenyl (PBB) "has by now entered the bodies of virtually all" of Michi-

gan's 9 million residents. He said the dangerous poison
"poses a lasting threat to human health. Blood, nervous
system, and immune system disorders and the long-range
threat of liver cancer are possibilities·for those who get
even minute amounts of PBB." The substance had been
accidentally mixed in with Michigan animal feed in 1973.

It seems that nothing is safe anymore. One chemical
used in over 100 hair dyes (4-methoxy-m-phenylenediame)
is now known to be carcinogenic, i.e., cancer producing.
One-half gram per year is absorbed into the blood in normal use. The chemical has no substitute and is considered
vital to the dyeing process (no pun intended). Because of
an exemption in the Federal law, the FDA cannot ban the
substance.[3] Red dye No. 2 and the artificial sweetener,
saccharin, are also carcinogenic, as is possibly its substitute, Wrigley's Xylitol.[4] A small listing of the more well
known poisonous chemicals around us include Mirex,
Kepone, PCB, DDT, PBB, PVC, PBCP, Dieldrin, and
there are others.

Environmental pollution is far more serious than most
people recognize, and there are a thousand different time
bombs around us, all waiting to go off. The earth has been
polluted and despoiled as in no other time in history.
The prophet Isaiah in the Bible, writing 700 years *before*
Christ, at some points seems to be writing about the coming Decade of Shock. He looked ahead and penned what
he saw:

> The earth mourns and withers, the world fades
> and withers, the exalted of the people of the earth
> fade away. The earth is also polluted by its
> inhabitants, for they transgressed laws, violated
> statutes, broke the everlasting covenant. There-
> fore a curse devours the earth, and those who
> live in it are held guilty. Therefore the inhabit-
> ants of the earth are burned, and few men are
> left . . . . The earth reels to and fro like a drunk-
> ard, and it totters like a shack, for its transgres-

sion is heavy upon it, and it will fall, never to rise again (Isa. 24:3-5, 20).

This passage goes on to refer to the return of the Lord to the earth in the last days (v. 23). It is both a time of severe judgment on man for his wickedness and the subsequent setting up of the Kingdom of God on earth. It is interesting to notice the pollution reference—it is as accurate as if it were written today.

CARCINOGENS

Chemical pollutants that produce cancer in animals also affect humans; authorities state there is a 100% correlation. In other words, if a substance causes cancer in animals, the chances are 100% it can do so in man.[5] Currently there are literally thousands of new chemicals developed and being developed, and most of them are expected to be cancer-producing. We used to be told to "eat an apple a day" for our health. Experts now state there will be "a new carcinogen a day," obviously something not so good for our health. In 1976, there were 350,000 new chemical substances of all types created.[6]

Many people assume carcinogenic test results are somewhat irrelevant, because massive doses are used, and that these are much more than is normally consumed. (The Xylitol tests involved a daily dose the equivalent of chewing six sticks of gum per hour, 16 hours a day.) However, this misses the point—to determine the long-term effect of a substance is what is important. Instead of waiting for 40 years of low level doses, the investigators use high level doses for a short period of time.

Another important factor is that we are not dealing with one chemical substance, for in fact we are dealing with hundreds and thousands of substances which are accumulating in our bones, tissues, brain, and internal organs. Our generation is the first in history having DDT, PCB's, and other organochlorine compounds in our tissues, fat, and liver, lead in our blood, mercury in our brains, potentially dangerous amounts of radioactive elements in our bones, asbestos particles in our lungs, and numerous other dangerous materials distributed throughout our bodies. Dr. Paul Ehrlich of Stanford states: "DDT alone may already have substantially reduced the statistical life expectancy of all of us, especially children born since 1948."[7]

THOUSANDS OF UNKNOWNS

Another very real problem of pollution is a problem of the unknown. For the majority of the thousands of new substances developed each year, we do not know the short-term impact or the long-term impact on either man or the environment. All we do know is that, despite the marvelous defense mechanisms of the human body, the more information that comes in, the bleaker things look.

According to Dr. Ehrlich, in areas where there are high concentrations of mercury pollution, microorganisms are currently converting it to a more dangerous form, methyl mercury, which causes brain damage. He tells us that methyl mercury can easily enter our food chains, and that even if no more mercury is discharged, there is enough stored in the bottom of some waters to keep adding methyl mercury to food chains in local areas for centuries ahead. He also makes the point that some scientists are greatly concerned with the quantities of lead found in the bodies of Americans. Sometimes the levels are approaching the point where they will be producing symptoms of chronic lead poisoning such as weakness, apathy, lowered fertility, and miscarriages. He also makes the point that exposure to lead was one of the factors in the decline of the Roman Empire.

Dr. Ehrlich tells us that pesticide horror stories are plentiful in the scientific literature. Dieldrin-resistant fish excrete so much of it that they kill nonresistant fish kept in the same tank.[8] There are already at least 75 pesticides alone which are restricted in use (in California) and should probably be banned.

The 40,000 different commercial pesticides are only a fraction of all currently toxic substances in use. Of six of the most recent considerations for restriction, two are 1,3 dichloropropene ("probably carcinogenic") and ethylene dibromide ("definitely carcinogenic"). Both are used on a wide variety of vegetable crops in California, which supplies much of the nation's needs. Another, carbon tetrachloride, is now known to "injure most cells in the body." Even though these substances are placed on a restricted list, it does not necessarily mean their use diminishes. It only requires that a permit is necessary to purchase it and that "a county agricultural commission can put conditions on its use."[9]

Actually the "war" against pesticides is being lost. Agricultural chemicals are a $5,000,000,000 a year business, and American agriculture is addicted to them. Due to monoculture (one-crop) farming and increasing insect resistance, American farmers have gone from using 100,000 pounds of pesticide a year in the 1940's to over one *billion* pounds a year in the 1970's, with Californian fields receiving over 10%.[10] Many pesticides also kill off the natural insect predators of the harmful variety, so demanding the use of more poison. This is all the more absurd when we discover that pesticides have not improved crop yields, and that farming organically produced nearly the same yields at less cost than chemical farming.[11] Even the national Academy of Sciences, in a 3 year 60-expert 5 volume study, concluded that toxic pesticides must be phased out because of environmental and health effects and their decreasing of crop yields, via the disruption of natural control mechanisms.[12]

In the opinion of Cornell University entomologist David Pimentel, the use of pesticides does little to improve crop yields. The point is made that U.S. farmers are still losing approximately the same percentage of their crops to insects that they lost before they began using chemical insecticides in the 1940's. At that time about 1% of the nation's corn crop was treated with insecticides, and bugs ate approximately 3% of the crops. In 1974 approximately 52% of the crop was sprayed and the insects devoured some 12% of the crop.[13] Obviously this would be true, not just in the

United States, but all over the world.[14]

HAVOC WITH HEALTH

Despite their ineffectiveness, their use continues, playing havoc with human health. According to the World Health Organization, at least 500,000 people suffer from pesticide poisoning annually (e.g., DBCP actually sterilized chemical workers in California). The U.S. EPA reports 14,000 pesticide poisonings a year, and some authorities say the unreported cases may be 100 times that number.[15] Some of the known cases involve periodic hospitalization as a way of life, resulting from Kepone poisoning—with symptoms including uncontrollable shaking, slurred speech, memory loss, sterility, and even cancer as a possible eventual result.[16]

As a result of working with the pesticide Leptophos, employees at the Velsicol Chemical Corp. in Bayport, Texas, suffered from partial paralysis, failures of muscular coordination, blurred vision, choking sensations, multiple sclerosis, and encephalitis.[17] As we approach the Decade of Shock we wonder what new physical, mental, and emotional problems will beset us.

PCB'S—THE HORSE HAS ALREADY BOLTED

Polychlorinated biphenyls (PCB's) are a good example of the type of problem we face. The danger was obvious over 5 years ago, but even today it is only just beginning to be recognized. Production may finally be banned but it will be far too late to stop the consequences resulting from the 1.4 billion pounds produced since 1929.

This is a classic case of shutting the gate after the proverbial horse has bolted. PCB's is a worse poison than DDT because it is more toxic and much more persistent in the environment and in humans. According to EPA studies over 90% of the people in this country have it in their tissues, and 5% of the population have levels that exceed guidelines for contaminated fish.[18]

It has been proved conclusively that PCB's are toxic to both man and animals. It affects a wide variety of farm animals from environmental (not test) contamination. The effects include reproductive failure, deformity, sickness, and even death. It has been estimated that 90% of all fresh water fish contain PCB's, 60% of them at levels of .5 ppm.

Mothers' milk may literally be no longer safe to drink. It already contained unacceptable levels of DDT, and now it has been found that it contains PCB's. It is startling to find that 79 of 80 women tested in 11 States by EPA had levels ranging from .2 ppm to 10.6 ppm. The letters ppm. stand for parts per million, this being the measurement showing how toxic these substances are. For example, according to the EPA, dioxin (which has been sprayed everywhere since 1948) kills laboratory animals and deforms their fetuses in the parts per *trillion* range.[19] A measurement of .5 ppm. PCB's causes reproductive failure in mink, according to U.S. Fish and Wildlife Service scientist, Chuck Walker.[20] A.K. Ahmed, Staff Scientist for the Natural Resources Defense Council in New York, states that with readings between 2.5 and 5.0 ppm., "severe reproductive failure" occurs in primates.[21] Compare this with the figure given above for 79 out of 80 women and we begin to see the seriousness of the situation. And this is only one of the world's problems as we approach the Decade of Shock.

It is a problem that should be taken very seriously. Dr. Norton Nelson, Director of The New York University Institute of Environmental Medicine, states: "If my wife had a baby, and if the PCB's were in the upper levels, certainly around four or five ppm. (in the milk fat), I would suggest that she *not* nurse."[22]

Part of the concern is the fact that some babies are now suckling near-toxic levels of PCB's, according to Joseph Highland of The Environmental Defense Fund.[23] Even babies who do not nurse are born with PCB's in their tissues. Research has shown that the poison is transferred to the baby through the placenta. In this connection the results of EPA tests are alarming, for PCB's were found for the first time in the embryonic fluid surrounding human fetuses as they developed and the concentrations were several times greater than the allowable safe limits.[24]

PROBLEMS FOR POTENTIAL MOTHERS

Highland further states: "We think PCB's are a very serious problem, not only for those consuming fish (one source of high concentrations) but for any potential mother in this country."[25]

David Zwerdling has a relevant article entitled "Chemical Catastrophes," published in *The Progressive* of February, 1977. He makes the point that PCB's are only the beginning of the chemical curse, and that in fact there are other toxins which EPA has recently found in breast milk—these are the cancer-causing chlorinated hydrocarbons such as dieldrin and heptachlor and the metabolites of chlordane and also kepone. He goes on to suggest that there are more than twenty known cancer-causing chemicals which we drink from the water we take from the kitchen tap. He makes the rather alarming statement that there are twenty known carcinogens from our ordinary water supply but that only about 10% of the 350 organic chemicals that are routinely found in such drinking water have ever been tested. Zwerdling goes on to say:

> And if the Government could muster so much concern over the one billion pounds of PCB's produced in all the years since the Great Depression, what about the truly significant industrial chemicals such as vinyl chloride and benzene? Industry produces sixteen billion pounds of these two cancer-causing chemicals—both are routinely found in air and water and vinyl chloride contaminates plastic-packaged foods—in a single year.[26]

Unfortunately, infants are more susceptible than adults to these poisons. Their bodies have not developed the capacity to metabolize and eliminate foreign substances very well, and because they weigh only 10% of an adult's weight, the same amount of poison has a worse effect on them.[27] If literally millions of turkeys, chickens, eggs, fish, and other foods have been destroyed because of PCB contamination alone, we can only wonder with alarm what we may be doing to our own children.[28]

Our concern is certainly justified when we remember that we are dealing with not just one substance, but thousands. When we deal with all kinds of toxic and potentially toxic chemicals, we find that the real horror story is a multiple one—that of quantity, toxicity, persistence in the environment, synergersic effects, delayed action effect, and bioaccumulatization.

In terms of quantity the $100 billion chemical industry has produced 34,000 chemical substances, and 2 million chemical mixtures are on the market. There are 1,000 new compounds made each year, according to the EPA.[29] Most chemicals on the market are "industrial trade secrets" so the vast majority never get tested, and no one knows how many are carcinogenic. We could be literally killing ourselves. The National Institute for Occupational Safety and Health has named some 1,500 commonly used chemicals as "suspected carcinogens," and perhaps this gives us some idea.[30]

Toxicity is another concern. If, as Dr. Ehrlich implies, DDT alone may have substantially reduced our lifetimes, then what are we to do with PCB's, which are more toxic? Or what about PBB's, another commonly used industrial chemical which is five times more toxic than PCB's? Or what about dioxin, which is even more deadly? As David Zwerdling points out, studies were completed recently by EPA, Harvard University, and Dow Chemical Company, confirming that there are substantial amounts of deadly dioxin contaminating the very beef we eat.

Dioxin kills laboratory animals at 600 parts per trillion or, .0006 parts per million. According to Dr. Matthew Meselson, Chairman of Biochemistry at Harvard, studies undertaken by personnel of the University of Wisconsin "suggest that, even if you're ingesting only a few parts per trillion of dioxin in beef (Harvard researchers found dioxin in 10% of beef samples tested, at levels as high as 60 ppt), then it may be only a matter of time before the accumulated dose reaches the toxic level . . . . No one knows what that level may be. But it could mean, perhaps in ten years, or perhaps in fifty, you might succumb to disease more easily, or develop chronic illness."[32]

One final pesticide (arsenic trioxide) should be mentioned, although it is not so commonly used. Dr. Petr Beckman of the University of Colorado points out that more of it is imported every year (by weight) "than all the nuclear wastes would amount to if all U.S. power were nuclear." Yet arsenic trioxide is 50 times as toxic as plutonium when ingested, and plutonium is a very deadly substance. "Arsenic trioxide is dispersed in random places on the earth's surface, mainly where food is grown. Long after the nuclear wastes have decayed to negligible levels, it will still be around in the biosphere."[33]

THE PERSISTENCE OF CHEMICALS

A major concern is the persistence of many of these chemicals and pesticides. This area has two aspects. First, once they enter ecosystems or human bodies, they do not simply break down and dissipate in a few months or years. They are chemically stable, and so they remain in the environment. Since they do not go away, they tend to accumulate in animals and man via food, air, and water, etc.

The second aspect is the percentage of manufactured, but as yet nonabsorbed contaminant. This is why stopping the production of a substance does not stop the danger. Indeed, the problem will continue for years, and it will get worse before it gets better. For example, in breaking down the location of the 1.4 billion pounds of PCB's the analysis is as follows:[34]

PCB's destroyed	4%
PCB's free in the environment	11%
PCB's in land fills	19%

Our current PCB problem stems from no more than

15% of all PCB's produced. The remaining 66% is in billions of items not yet discarded, much of which will eventually reach the ecosystems.

> All the evidence suggests that the PCB threat will not get better in our lifetimes, it will probably get worse. Congress may have voted to ban production of the chemical within the next two years, but the nation did not ban the use of PCB's. And while the PCB's in our bodies and in our food are the legacy of only 150 million pounds of the chemical leaked into the environment since 1930, there are 750 *million more pounds* still available and being used.[35]

Another factor is synergisms—combinational effects. This is really an unknown area since so little research has been done. However, it is known that two substances can chemically combine, to make a more deadly chemical than the sum of their parts.

The potential exists for serious developments in the future, and these might ultimately be more dangerous than we suspect. For example, it is possible that nitric oxide, nitrogen dioxide, nitrous acid, and four kinds of amines react together in the air to form carcinogenic nitrosamines. Separately the substances are simple pollutants or chemical compounds.[36]

THE DELAYED ENVIRONMENTAL
ACTION EFFECT

The next important factor is what we call the Delayed Environmental Action Effect. As mentioned earlier, even if all chemical and pesticide production were stopped today, the contaminated effect on man and his living environment would increase for many years, even possibly decades. Various pollutants are widely distributed throughout ecosystems, and they take time to accumulate in living tissue. However, the important issue here is that there are so many substances, so little research, and so few are restricted in use or are banned, that, because of continued production and use, the effects 20 years down the road will be much more severe than they are today. Many of the substances do not break down easily in the body, but they remain and accumulate. A steady or increasing absorption from the environment could have serious consequences many years ahead.

The next factor is the cumulative effect in the living ecosystems, and this involves the food chain. One reason why the brown pelican nearly became extinct was because it ate fish with high levels of DDT, and this interfered with its calcium production. As concentrations were increased in the birds, the egg shells laid were so thin that they were unable to support the life within. What had happened was that, as one ascended up the food chain from phytoplankton to fish to pelican, concentrations of DDT greatly increased, because each predator required a certain amount of prey to sustain itself. The poisons became concentrated as they passed along the food chains.

All the above factors combine to give us some idea of the magnitude of the problem, and it is not confined to the U.S. There are similar problems all over the world, particularly in relatively advanced technological-industrial countries.

However, even "backward" countries are suffering from pesticide poisoning. For example, in India, where the amount of pesticides used is relatively low, we still find "about one third of the food an Indian eats contains pesticide residues in quantities exceeding permitted tolerance levels," and that samples of breast milk of women in Guatemala and El Salvador show a contamination *20 to 70 times* higher than the limits established by the World Health Organization for maximum tolerance level in cows' milk.[37]

Thus, for one nation to stop pesticide production would not do much, for we are looking at a global ecosystem, and chemical pollution is only one of scores of other pollution-environmental problems.

THE INCREASE OF CANCER
TO ONE IN FOUR?

It is now being recognized that admittedly low, but repeated doses of commonplace pollutants are a positive factor in disease. A late 1975 Library of Congress Report— "Effects of Chronic Exposure to Low Level Pollutants in the Environment"— documented the fact that toxic substances accumulate in the body and increase the chances of illness, damaging genes, causing cancer, heart disease, respiratory disease, and damaging the nervous system. Some of the culprits are asbestos, chlorines, fluorides, nickel, and mercury, most of which enter the water and air via the industrial processes.

The Report also disclosed:

1. Complicated and expensive testing methods are not sensitive enough to detect polluting agents, hence only a portion of the chemically induced health damage can be detected.
2. Costs to society of pollution diseases are staggering.
3. Environmental problems may account for 70% to 90% of the causes of cancer and heart disease.[38]

Heart disease and cancer are the No. 1 and No. 2 killers of Americans today, and at its current rate of development cancer will develop in 1 out of 4 people.[39]

Current funding to test the possible toxicity of thousands of new substances is so low that for all practical purposes nothing is being done. We will simply have to wait. Some people, however, are not optimistic. Stanford Biologist, Dr. Paul Ehrlich states:

> Contrary to what most people think, the biggest pollution problems are not the direct assaults on human beings. Now those direct assaults are serious enough. Things like chlorinated hydrocarbons, DDT and other pesticides, PCB's and so on, and other poisons that we are treating ourselves to, may very well shorten our life expectancy considerably: it could even reduce it

from 65 years to 30 years . . . . The really serious problem is the assaults that these chemicals and other things that human beings do, the effects that they have on the ecosystems, the life support systems of our planet, which recycle our wastes, supply us with all our food from the sea, control most of our crop pests, and so on. If we destroy those systems, then we won't have any life expectancy at all for many human beings, and things will really be disastrous.[40]

A WORLDWIDE ECOLOGICAL CATASTROPHE WITHIN A GENERATION

Jacques Cousteau stated in 1975:

If I live as long as my father (24 more years) I fully expect to witness the first worldwide ecological catastrophe.[41]

He predicts the possibility of this catastrophe as "100 percent certain." He still wants to warn others, however, because "maybe nine out of 10 will die. But if we can save even 20 or 30 million (of 6 billion), well, that's something."[42]

Those in the world today who really understand what is happening are the ones who are terrified. After 1,000 hours of research into the predicament of modern man, your present authors join those who recognize that humanly speaking there is no hope. However, we do see hope— for our conviction is that God is still in control, still interested in the affairs of men, and He will be seen to overcome all problems in a coming age.

There are other aspects touching our ecological systems, and we turn to those in the next chapter.

Footnotes: Chapter 11

1. "60 Minutes" News broadcast November 13, 1977, Channel 2, Los Angeles.
2. *Newsweek,* September 27, 1976, p. 39.
3. "Chemical Used In Hair Dyes Identified As Carcinogen," *Los Angeles Times,* November 17, 1977; "60 Minutes" News Broadcast, November 13, 1977, Ch. 2.
4. *Ibid.*
5. "60 Minutes News Broadcast," November 13, 1977, Channel 2.
6. *Ibid.; Los Angeles Times,* Dec. 26, 1977.
7. Paul Ehrlich, *How To Be A Survivor* (New York: Ballantine, 1971), p. 5.
8. *Ibid.,* p. 34.
9. "Pesticide Causes Cancer, Hearing Told," *Los Angeles Times,* October 26, 1977.
10. *Ibid.*
11. "Organic Farmer Protects Soil For Future," *Los Angeles Times,* December 2, 1972.
12. Pest Control: An Assessment of Present and Alternative Technologies, Printing and Publishing Office, NAS, 2101 Constitution Ave., N.W., Washington, DC 20418.
13. "Pesticide Causes Cancer," *Los Angeles Times,* October 26, 1977.
14. *Ibid.*
15. *Ibid.*
16. *Newsweek,* September 27, 1976, p. 39; Daniel Zwerdling "Chemical Catastrophes," *The Progressive,* February, 1977, p. 16.
17. *Ibid.*
18. Stuart Diamond, "PCB Could Be Chemical Scare of 1970's," *Los Angeles Times,* November 24, 1977.
19. Daniel Zwerdling, "Chemical Catastrophes," *The Progressive,* February, 1977, pp. 17-18.
20. *Ibid.*
21. A. Karim Ahmed, "PCB's In The Environment," *Environment,* March, 1976, p. 9.

22. Ibid., pp. 16-17.
23. *Ibid.*, pp. 15-16.
24. *Ibid* and *Los Angeles Times,* November 24, 1977.
25. *Los Angeles Times, Ibid.*
26. "Chemical Catastrophes," *The Progressive,* February, 1977, p. 18.
27. Joseph Highland, "PCB's In Food," *Environment,* March, 1976, pp. 15-16.
28. *Ibid.*, p. 14.
29. Zwerdling, "Chemical Catastrophes," *The Progressive,* February, 1977, pp. 16-17.
30. *Ibid.*
31. *Ibid.*, p. 18.
32. *Ibid.*
33. Petr Beckman, *The Health Hazards Of NOT Going Nuclear* (Boulder, CO, The Golem Press, 1976) p. 102.
34. *Los Angeles Times,* November 24, 1977.
35. *The Progressive,* February, 1977, p. 18.
36. George Alexander, "Pollutants Mixed With Air Form Carcinogens in Lab," *Los Angeles Times,* October 25, 1977.
37. *Ceres,* January-February, 1976, pp. 10-11.
38. *Los Angeles Times,* November 9, 1975.
39. Gerald O. Barney, *The Unfinished Agenda* (New York: Thomas Crowell Co., 1977) pp. 92-3.
40. Unused Portion Of Interview By Robert Amran (1976) for film *The Late Great Planet Earth,* used by permission of Dr. Ehrlich.
41. Interview, *People,* September 15, 1975.
42. *Ibid.*

Chapter 12

POLLUTION OF THE OCEAN AND RIVERS

There are many other significant pollution-related changes occurring in our ecological systems (ecosystems), and these changes may profoundly affect our lives individually and collectively. One example is the ocean.

THE WORLD'S DUMPING GROUND

The ocean has long been the world's dumping ground for every type of poison or waste imaginable. Most pollutants eventually find their way to the oceans via rivers, etc., and the problem of pollution has become so serious that some professionals are stating the oceans will die within decades.

In *People's Weekly* and *National Enquirer* interviews Jacques Cousteau was quoted as stating that we pour so many millions of tons of poisonous waste into the sea that in perhaps less than 20 years the oceans will have received their mortal wound and will actually start to die. He goes on to suggest that if the oceans did die all life would soon end—not only marine life but all other animals and plants of the earth, including man.

Cousteau estimates that the vitality of the seas, in terms of fish and plant life, declined 50% in the 20 years prior to 1971.

HORRORS TO FOLLOW
THE DEATH OF MARINE LIFE

Cousteau believes that when "the pyramid of life collapses," (that fragile food chain linking phytoplankton to man), so do we.[1] When the oceans die and the marine life rots, the surface will be covered with decaying matter, preventing cloud formation over the oceans and causing worldwide droughts and resultant famines.[2] Because of oxygen depletion, "life will be impossible within 50 miles of the coasts." He says, "I beg you not to dismiss this brief scenario as science fiction. The ocean can die, these horrors can happen."[3]

Another quotation, this time from the Biblical Book of the Revelation (8:8-9), seems relevant:

> The second angel blew his trumpet, and something resembling a great mountain, blazing with fire, was hurled into the sea.

> And a third of the sea was turned to blood, a third of the living creatures in the sea perished, and a third of the ships were destroyed.

Maybe the apostle John, the writer of the Revelation, was pointing to our coming Decade of Shock, for he speaks only of one-third of the fish dying. Cousteau estimates it will be 20 years before they *all* die.

Jacques Piccard is another who warns that unless something is done the oceans will be dead before the end of the century.[4]

One of the reasons for concern is that 90% of all marine life in the ocean exists above the continental shelves next to the land—and that is the portion of the oceans where the pollutants are being dumped and concentrated.[5] This area represents much less than ½ of 1% of ocean space, yet it contains the vast majority of marine life.

Here are some examples of what we put into our oceans.

French rivers carry 18 billion cubic meters of liquid pollution into the sea each year. In the Federal Republic of Germany, 9 billion cubic meters are dumped each year. In the U.S., smoke and noxious fumes alone put 390,000 tons of pollutants into the air every *day* (142,000,000 tons per year), much of which eventually finds its way to the ocean.[6] Around the world, 1½ billion pounds of pesticides are used yearly. Such pesticides, oil spills, and hundreds of thousands of chemicals and other products are all part of the oceans' problem.

Thor Heyerdahl estimates that, were it not for ocean currents, life on the continental shelves would have been exterminated or severely decimated long ago.[7] He says that hardly a creek or river in the world exists where it is safe to drink from the outlet, and nearly every river carries "a constant flow of nondegradable chemicals from industrial, urban, or agricultural areas" to the ocean. As Heyerdahl says, "A dead ocean means a dead planet,"[8] and many of these poisons are extremely toxic—1 part per billion of PCB's in water kills 50% of exposed shrimp within 15 days.[9]

World fish catches have been declining in recent years, for the first time in decades.[10] Pollution levels on the Russian Atlantic Ocean are already beyond tolerable safe limits, and, as with Los Angeles and other smog cities, the "tolerable" limits had to be revised upward.

People do not realize how "linked" everything is. The environment is a unified ecosystem—there are important links between terrestrial, aquatic, and atmospheric ecosystems.[11] Pollutants that go into one system eventually find their way into oceans, and as a result their fish become polluted, then the fish in turn are eaten by man, and he also becomes polluted.

These ecosystems are so delicately intertwined that insecticide pollution in Utah affects fish production in Scotland.[12] Nor are the links limited to environmental matters—they are extended to economic, social, and political arenas. There are occasional extreme cases, e.g., where environmental concerns for a three-inch minnow has blocked completion of the $400 million Little Ten-nessee River dam,[13] but the typical cases are the most serious.

One example is that grave risk from mercury pollution in the Mediterranean Sea is threatening its $700 million annual catch. There are 100 million people who live along its shores and an equal number of tourists who visit each year. However, inhabitants and tourists alike now run grave risks to their health, primarily from sewage. Health horror tales are common, including cases of cholera traced to contaminated mussels that have been sold on the black market.

A meeting of 13 involved nations who wanted to clean up the Mediterranean was abandoned, because the *initial* cost was 5 billion dollars, compounded by the necessity for a blacklist of river dumping-radioactive wastes, mineral oils, mercury, DDT, PCB's and other organochlorine compounds which would be prohibitively costly and would affect the health and well-being of numerous industries and cities.[14] The fact is, the Mediterranean is going the way of Lake Erie, and so is the ocean, although at a slower pace.

Ten years ago no nation on earth was especially con-cerned with the possibility of polluting the "limitless" ocean. No nation bothered to lay claim to more than a 3-mile limit. Today, with recognition that the oceans' resources are being depleted by pollution and over-fishing, nations are laying claim to all the mileage they can get, usually 200 miles. Prodded by food shortages, nations are grabbing for fish wherever they can get them—often thousands of miles away from home. The Law of the Sea Conference, an attempt to solve current problems, has largely failed. After 7 years of conferences, little has been accomplished and nations "have been more concerned with national pride, national rights, and national re-sources, than the 'common heritage' concept."[15]

According to *The National Academy of Sciences,* there has been another consequence as well. "Unless changes are made in the Revised Single Negotiating Text, the forthcoming Law of the Sea will cripple future marine scientific research, which will be critical to the survival of the oceans and mankind.''[16]

OXYGEN DEPLETION

There is another relevant factor in ocean pollution. In an address to the American Association for the Advancement of Science, Professor Cole pointed out that 70% or more of the total oxygen production by photosynthesis occurs in the ocean, and that it is largely produced by planktonic diatoms. He reminds his listeners that vast quantities of pollutants are being dumped into the ocean, and that one estimate by the U.S. Food and Drug Administration suggests that as many as a half-million substances are involved. Cole points out that many of these are biologically active, including pesticides, radioisotopes, and detergents, to which the living forms of earth have never had to adapt. Only a minute fraction of them have been tested for toxicity to marine diatoms or other forms of life involved in the cycles of nitrogen and other essential elements. He spoke of possible disaster, and pointed out also that both DDT and mercury inhibit photosynthesis in planktonic plants.[17]

Most people think we will have long since destroyed ourselves by other means before our oxygen runs out, but there are other possible consequences of poisoning plankton. Among them are large changes in plankton communities, resulting in catastrophic losses for fisheries, leading to further world food depletion.[18]

TAP WATER TOO!

Recent National Research Council studies are relevant in another area. They indicate that bacteriological standards now in use for U.S. drinking water do not necessarily provide adequate protection against waterborne diseases, particularly from reclaimed waste water.[19] Another report, commissioned by the National Center for Health Statistics, found that outbreaks of diseases related to drinking water doubled from 1966-70 to 1971-74.[20]

However, let us conclude by a further reference to the sea. In general, man tends not to take the threat to ocean life too seriously. For most people, the ocean is a place to visit, and fish are simply an alternative form of food. We live on the land and are not yet made uncomfortable by problems associated with the seas.

Nevertheless the years are rushing by, and the last decade has witnessed significant changes in the patterns of ocean life. There have been mysterious cases of "mass suicide"— so it was thought—of fish populations, and dangerous levels of mercury poisoning have been reported as far away as Australia. The world is not divorced from its oceans, but is in fact connected by them.

And the oceans are dying. Our birth pains associated with the Decade of Shock are at the same time the death throes of many of our ocean-living contemporaries. The struggles are proceeding simultaneously. Life and death move together, and the two are related more closely than you and I like to think.

Footnotes: Chapter 12

1. Jacques Cousteau, *National Enquirer,* October 12, 1974; *People Weekly,* Sept. 15, 1975, pp. 28-9.
2. "Dying Oceans, Poisoned Seas," *Time,* November 8, 1971, p. 74.
3. Jacques Cousteau, *National Enquirer,* October 12, 1974, and *People Weekly*, September 15, 1975, pp. 28-9.
4. *Time,* Nov. 8, 1971, note 2.
5. Thor Heyerdahl, "Polluting The Ocean," *Current,* January, 1976, pp. 52-53.
6. *Ibid.,* p. 54.
7. *Ibid.*
8. *Ibid.*
9. *Los Angeles Times,* November 24, 1977; Lestor Brown, *Los Angeles Times,* December 4, 1977.

10. Heyerdahl, *Current,* January, 1976, p. 56.
11. G.E. Likens, F.H. Bormann, "Linkages Between Terrestrial and Aquatic Ecosystems," *Bioscience,* August, 1974, p. 447.
12. Paul Ehrlich, *The Population Bomb,* p. 35.
13. *Los Angeles Times,* November 15, 1977.
14. "$5 Billion Tab Stalls Treaty on Mediterranean Environment," *Los Angeles Times,* October 22, 1977.
15. *News Report,* August, 1977, p. 1; *Los Angeles Times,* September 2, 1976; E. Leeper, "Many Issues, Few Agreements For Law Of The Sea," *Bioscience,* March, 1976, pp. 173-6.
16. *News Report, Ibid.,* p. 3.
17. Paul Ehrlich, *The Population Bomb,* p. 41.
18. *Ibid.,* p. 36.
19. *News Report,* August, 1977, p. 1.
20. *Los Angeles Times,* December 7, 1977, Part 1, p. 2.

Chapter 13

POLLUTION OF THE ATMOSPHERE

Death rates from both emphysema and lung cancer have risen spectacularly over the last decade, especially among urban populations. [Air] pollution also may be linked with certain kinds of heart disease and tuberculosis, not as a cause but as a contributing factor. In addition to this disease threat, there is also the strong suspicion that occurrence of certain cancers is associated with specific pollutants in the air.[1]

EXPERIMENTS WITH HUMAN LUNG CELLS

As more evidence accumulates, it becomes obvious that air pollution is a contributing factor to disease and death. In new experiments which allow human lung cells to survive outside the body, it has been found that the cells are more sensitive than suspected. According to a team of University of California (Irvine) scientists, lung cells are "extraordinarily sensitive" to *low* levels of nitrogen dioxide, a common component of smog.[2] Less than 4% of the cells survived a six hour exposure to .15 ppm of nitrogen dioxide. The research "does provide data showing that nitrogen dioxide is in fact a highly toxic gas that can be lethal at the concentrations found in smog."[3]

The *Los Angeles Times* recently noted the conclusions of a group of 75 scientists, sponsored by the Energy Research and Development Administration. They stated that the burning of coal, oil, and gas may be threatening our atmosphere, and that a variety of other energy sources must be kept available. The burning of fossil fuels could double the amount of carbon dioxide in the air over the next 50-75 years, which could increase world temperatures by more than 4° or 5° Fahrenheit. "The report said that carbon dioxide from fuel burning could cause such severe effects that it will have to be stopped or reduced very quickly."[4]

The problem here is that other energy sources are not available and will not be available for a long time. A 4° or 5° rise in world temperatures would be catastrophic, to both climate and crops alike.

THE IMPORTANCE OF OZONE

The potential harm of reducing the earth's ozone layer is so significant that the Pentagon has actually considered military strategy, involving detonating a nuclear bomb in space directly above enemy countries. The idea would be to remove the ozone shield, and expose the occupants below to direct ultraviolet radiation, which is deadly to all forms of life.[5] According to Jim Martzler of the Arms Control and Disarmament Agency, the effect could be more dangerous than atomic fallout.[6]

However, it seems that we do not need an atomic bomb after all. A common ingredient in aerosol sprays is fluorocarbon, and it is nearly certain that it has been found to deplete the ozone layer which blocks out 99% of the sun's deadly radiation. Without that ozone shield, life could not exist.

Dr. Ralph Cicerone, of Michigan's Space Physics Research Laboratory, states concerning this problem, that "it is the most serious environmental problem we have yet identified."[7]

Ron Chernov notes that:

> Even normally cautious scientists are scripting science-fiction scenarios that could follow ozone depletion late in this century: a startling increase in the rate of skin cancer, vast and possibly devastating shifts in global weather, cataclysmic disruptions of the food chain. In short, they fear that depletion of the fragile ozone layer would so perilously tip the ecological balance that it would take the planet decades—or longer—to recover.[8]

"DOOMSDAY IN 25 YEARS"

The more recent estimates (assuming present production trends and use) indicate that 7% to 20% of the ozone shield could be depleted by the year 2,000.[9] However, this figure depends on certain factors. It could be as much as 30% by 1994.[10] What would this mean? Thomas M. Donahue of the Atmospheric Science Department at the University of Michigan says it would mean doomsday, the end of life on earth: "We are talking about the end of the world—doomsday in 25 years . . . certainly the end of mankind."[11]

As with so many other cases of environmental problems, the situation goes beyond fluorocarbons to economics. If we ban all production, a $9 billion job industry suffers the consequences, and so does the U.S. economy. If we go on as we have been going, we can be certain of at least a 10% reduction, for the fluorocarbons do not break down (their atmospheric life times are 40-150 years) and would continue to seep up to the stratosphere for a decade, even if production were stopped today.

INCREASE OF CANCER AND CLIMATE CHANGES

According to Dr. F. S. Rowland, this 10% reduction could cause anywhere from a 25% to 60% increase in cases of skin cancer per year, or 200,000 to 500,000 new cases per year in the U.S. alone.[12] It was originally thought that the worst effect was the increase in skin cancer, but now it appears possible that the dramatic effect to our climate may be even worse. There are also potentially serious effects on some food crops and the oceanic phytoplankton. These effects result just from fluorocarbons, but SST's deplete the ozone layer as well. (A fleet of 500 SST's would produce a 50% increase in nitrous oxides and might reduce the ozone by 10% to 20% within 5 to 10 years.)[13] Fluorocarbons reduce ozone 6 times faster than nitrous oxide.

Current U.S. and Russian military strategy allows for the limited use of nuclear weapons. The evidence indicates that nuclear explosions also deplete ozone so that, in the words of *Science* magazine, "There now appears to be additional reasons to regard even limited nuclear war as a potentially global catastrophe."[14]

Dr. Harold Johnston of U.C. Berkeley estimates there was a 3% to 6% reduction in ozone in the Northern Hemisphere during the heavy atomic testing years of 1961-62. It took 2½ years for natural regenerating mechanisms to restore half the loss. (The amount of ozone present fluctuates irregularly, apparently with sunspot cycles.)

Carbon tetrachloride as well as fluorocarbons have already each removed 1% of the ozone shield, according to estimates by Dr. Rowland of U.C. Irvine.[15] Who knows what the other tens of thousands of industrial chemicals now in use are doing to our atmosphere?

HALOCARBONS: EFFECTS ON STRATOSPHERIC OZONE

For at least 10 years, ozone depletion will continue, according to the National Research Councils. We will have to wait to find out what fluorocarbons (used in spray cans) will do to our atmosphere, regardless of a ban on production.[16] Any production curtailment must be worldwide to be effective—the U.S. produces only about 38% of the most commonly used fluorocarbons.[17]

However, a more immediate hazard is spray cans themselves: deliberate inhaling of the gases from spray cans can cause death, and small repeated exposure has been shown to be potentially dangerous. By 1973, resulting from the sniffing of fluorocarbons for a "high", over 140 young people had died from cardiac arrest.[18]

The use of spray cans containing the propellant vinyl chloride, now known to be carcinogenic, will under normal use in a house produce "400 times the safe level of exposure for workers," according to the Department of Labor's Occupational Safety and Health Administration.[19]

Whether or not this is coincidental, the incidence of malignant melanoma (a skin cancer fatal in 30% of cases) has been increasing from 5% to 10% a year, according to Dr. Thomas B. Fitzpatrick of Harvard Medical School.[20]

INCREASED ULTRAVIOLET RADIATION

There are other possible serious effects, including upsetting the balance of aquatic life and affecting some insect populations which play crucial roles in various ecosystems. A. K. Ahmed, staff scientist at the Natural Resources Defense Council, Inc., New York, states that it is not known to what extent ultraviolet radiation may upset the balance of aquatic life, but that significant effects might occur in certain aquatic environments where marine life is most productive. He includes estuaries and intertidal coastal regions as environments where such effects might occur.[21]

A 50% reduction in the ozone layer could increase temperatures worldwide by ½ degree C., which could cause chaos in the world agricultural system via climatic shifts following the melting of vast amounts of sea ice.[22]

Dr. V. Ramanathan, of NASA's Langley Research Center, has done research on fluorocarbon-climatic effects. According to *The New Scientist* of October 2, 1975:

> The results of his calculations, due to be published in *Science*, are ominous. Fluorocarbons have a "greenhouse" effect that will warm the earth by enough to cause significant climatic changes—including perhaps melting the polar ice caps—if their concentration in the atmosphere

increases from the present .1 parts per thousand million to one or two parts per thousand million. And R. Peck, a General Motors physicist, has found that "ozone profile changes (the amount of ozone at different altitudes) theoretically could influence temperature more strongly than even severe ozone depletion."[23]

Nitrogen based fertilizers may also deplete ozone.[24]

Fluorocarbons constitute about 4% of total halocarbon production in the U.S.—these include chloroform, ethylene, dichloride, etc. No one knows what effect, if any, these could be having. The case is as Dr. Rowland states: "Delays now in restricting fluorocarbon production will extract a cruel penalty from several generations to come."[25]

The subject is huge, and would justify a separate book, touching on many other aspects of pollution. The world is becoming increasingly aware of the dangers inherent in pollution, partly because of personal overtones.

In scientific circles today there is serious discussion and recognition of the dangers inherent in pollution. The problems facing the world are being considered realistically, perhaps most vociferously by a younger generation that will pay the penalty if they do not insist upon certain actions. They may not be entirely successful in their ambitious objectives, but at least there is active awareness of the seriousness of a whole series of interlocking problems that are already at crisis level.

Footnotes: Chapter 13

1. Ehrlich, *The Population Bomb,* p. 37.
2. "Smog Deadly To Lung Cells, Study Shows," *Los Angeles Times,* December 3, 1977.
3. *Ibid.*
4. *Los Angeles Times,* December 5, 1977, Part 1, p. 2.
5. "Peaceful Era In Space May End Soon," *The Futurist,* June, 1977, p. 191.
6. *Philadelphia Enquirer,* December 8, 1974.
7. *Ibid.*
8. *Philadelphia Enquirer,* December 8, 1974, p. 30 (Today): *Science,* October 8, 1976, "The Ozone Layer: The Threat From Aerosol Cans Is Real," p. 170.
9. Dr. F.S. Rowland, "In His Own Worlds," *People Weekly,* October 18, 1976; *Chemical and Engineering News,* May, 1976, p. 13.
10. M. Drosnin, "What's Being Done About Those Killer Aerosol Cans—Nothing," *New Times,* 1974, p. 28; Walter Sullivan, *New York Times,* September 26, 1974, p. 27, "Stratospheric Pollution: Multiple Threats To Earth's Ozone," *Science,* October 25, 1974.
11. *Ibid.,* Drosnin, p. 28.
12. F.S. Rowland, "Recent Studies Give Support To Ozone Depletion Theory," *Food and Drug Packaging,* July 15, 1976, Vol. 35, No. 2; "Chlorofluorocarbons Threaten Ozone Layer," *(Chemical And Engineering News),* September 23, 1974, p. 27; *Philadelphia Enquirer,* December 8, 1974; *New Yorker,* April 7, 1975.
13. *Science,* October 25, 1974, p. 336.
14. *Ibid.,* p. 337.
15. *Philadelphia Enquirer,* December 8, 1974.
16. *Halocarbons: Effects On Stratospheric Ozone,* National Academy Of Sciences, Washington, D.C. 1976, p. 162.
17. Walter Sullivan, *The New York Times,* September 18, 1976.
18. *Ibid., Philadelphia Enquirer,* December 8, 1974.

19. Paul Brodew, *New Yorker,* April 7, 1975.
20. "Flurocarbon-Use Limit Urged," *The Wall Street Journal,* September 14, 1976.
21. J. Eigner, "Unshielding The Sun . . . Environmental Effects," and A. Ahmed, "Unshielding The Sun . . . Human Effects," *Environment,* April-May, 1975.
22. *Ibid.*
23. *Science News,* May 8, 1976.
24. *Wall Street Journal,* December 3, 1975, p. 17.
25. *Los Angeles Times,* April 27, 1975.

Chapter 14

ECONOMIC CONDITIONS: WORLD

In 1923 Germany's problems were largely confined to that one nation, at a time when nation-states were largely independent. Today, they are interdependent. With advances in communications and technology, conditions have arisen which increasingly tend to make the world one large nation-state. This is as true economically as it is environmentally. Alvin Toffler points out:

> Today the entire industrial world is caught in a violent inflationary spiral that spares no one. The economic system has become overly interdependent, so that there are no innocent bystanders. This means, as well, that in the event of collapse, there will be fewer external sources of new capital to pull us out.[1]

"Stagflation" (inflation with economic stagnation) is common all over the world, and even the most respected of observers and experts entertain thoughts of economic doom.

Leonard Silk, a chief economic writer of the *New York Times,* puts forward the argument that the world has been slow to realize that we are living in the shadow of one of the greatest economic catastrophes known in modern history. He suggests that the world economy is threatened with breakdown and disintegration, with monetary disorder affecting the whole of the non-communist world.[2]

"PERHAPS AS EARLY AS 1979"

Senator Jacob Javits, in a *Newsweek* interview (September 26, 1977), stated that the massive oil debts that countries are building up all over the world could trigger "a severe (global) depression, perhaps as early as 1979."[2] That is awfully close to the Decade of Shock.

Ashby Bladon, a senior financial executive of the Guardian Life Insurance Company, put forward the argument that it would be practically impossible to return to either price stability or to financial stability without there being an intervening crash. He argues that if the crash is postponed by continuing an inflationary process with excessive credit expansion, the crash itself will be so much the worse when it does come. He argues that this is a worldwide threat that has been seriously added to by the enormous deficits incurred by oil-producing nations.[3]

Dr. Robert A. Gordon, President of the American Economic Association and Professor at U.C. Berkeley comments: "I don't think we have a body of economic theories that are of great help in today's world."[4]

NO MORE LENDING

The Third World must have more money in order to survive, for their problems in relation to poverty, famines, etc., are much worse than ours. Not only do they need money to survive, but they are *demanding* it. They want the cancellation of all debts incurred so far (multi-tens of billions), and billions more in no-interest loans and handouts. The problem is critical in Third World countries, with many of them going deeper into debt because of higher prices for oil. They must have the money, but the money just is not there to give.

UPI business writer John Sims had an article in the *Los*

Angeles Times of October 3rd, 1977, entitled "U.S. Banks May Be Near Limit On Third World Aid." He argues that the years 1978 and 1979 might well be critical for poorer countries of the world, and that America's commercial banks could be what he calls at the eye of the storm, whether they like it or not. He further makes the point that developing countries without oil of their own will run a $38.9 billion trade deficit in 1978, and by the end of that year will have amassed $253 billion in debts, this being an estimate put out by the United Nations Trade & Development Agency.

Without changes in the debt situation of the world's developing countries, we may be heading for a global depression that will make the 1930's look like a golden era of prosperity.[5] A late 1977 global money conference involving 3,000 "grim and serious" delegates from 131 countries concluded the world is beginning to realize "it lives in one finite economy."[6] The conference stated that the rich nations must be the ones to renew economic growth, but that a world economic slump could be ahead because the "big three," U.S., West Germany, and Japan, would not be able to do enough to prevent it.

NORTH-SOUTH PROBLEMS

The problem is largely between the North (developed) countries and those of the South (developing). Developing countries export 3 to 4 times more to industrialized countries than to each other. Because oil is four times as expensive today as it was five years ago, four times as much products must be used to purchase the same amount. Hence countries who do not have the money, borrow it, thus increasing their debt. Between 1968 and 1973 *before* the oil price raise, national debts to foreign countries increased as follows:[7]

S. Europe	96.9%
Asia	108.9%
Latin America	109.6%
Africa	115.1%

With the energy crises, debts have increased proportionately and the ability to repay has gone almost entirely. Willy Brandt, former West German Chancellor, concerned by the failure of 18 months of economic discussions in Paris, agreed to try to end the deadlock between North-South countries. Despite many other duties, he took the job due to his "conviction that peace in the world . . . even the survival of mankind" depends on resolving the conflict.[8]

Note the significance of the following interview between Senator Jacob Javits and *Newsweek*.[9] Bible students might notice certain Biblical implications in his solution. (De Borchgrave is the interviewer.)

Q. What is the chain of events you feel could lead to a global depression in two to three years?

A. Cessation of new lending by Western banks to the non-oil-producing developing countries. Our banks today are pretty well all loaned up. This could bring about an enormous credit squeeze that would be a shock the world monetary system could not absorb.

Q. Do you anticipate something as severe as the Great Depression of the 1930's?

A. Absolutely. And interestingly enough, it would have the same cause—bank-credit stringency. The banks will simply be unable to extend the kind of credit needed to keep the system going. And the international banking institutions will not have the wherewithal to pick up the slack.

Q. What has to be done to avoid such a depression?

A. The solution must be political and diplomatic. It will, by definition, involve a large amount of risk-taking and require the kind of leadership that is now sadly lacking all over the Western world, including the U.S. We need strict arms-limitation agreements, greater investment by the

oil-producing nations, and the political union of
West Europe.

Where would such a political union lead? It would bear
remarkable resemblance to the Roman Empire of New
Testament times—an empire that many students of prophecy believe must be revived, as foretold by the prophet
Daniel.

Communist countries currently owe the West over $60
billion. Repayment would help ease the difficulty, but that
would collapse their own system and would upset their
plans that are aimed at the economic disruption of the
West.[10]

A recent U.N. study, "The Future of the World Economy," found that the rich-poor gap could be narrowed
"only if developing nations devote 30% to 40% of their
gross national product to capital investment," that land
productivity must be increased by 60% to 100%, and
that "enormous efforts must be made to reform institutions in both the rich and poor nations in order to attain
the goals."[11] Practically speaking, the above requirements
are not only unfeasible, they are impossible, for reasons
we shall discuss as we proceed.

Current world economic conditions are extremely
serious. It is submitted that the claim must be taken
seriously, that only a world dictator, with full authority
and control over the multitudinous interweaving complex
social-political-economic systems and factors, could
achieve a world of stability. As conditions continue to
deteriorate, it is likely that the people and their leaders
everywhere will welcome his advent. He will appear to
have the solutions that the world needs so desperately.
With military and political tensions between East and
West, economic tensions between North and South, and
the world's people lost in uncertainty, he will come, and
he will be welcomed.

It is relevant to notice the words of Paul Henry Spaak:
he served as first President of the Council of Europe,
was one of the planners of the European Common Mar-

ket, is a former President of the U.N. General Assembly, Secretary-General of NATO, Belgium's Minister of Foreign Affairs, and Prime Minister of his own nation. He has written:

> Send us a man who can hold the allegiance of all the people, and whether he be God or the devil we will receive him.[12]

In a time of moral, religious, economic, and leadership vacuums, as Dostoevsky's devil states, "Once humanity has renounced God . . . the man-god will make his appearance."[13]

The Decade of Shock will clearly have drastic impacts on our economic life, our political life, our religious life, and virtually every other area of human life. The realization of our enforced involvement is becoming more intense as the economic pressures bear down on us everywhere—West, East, North, South, and Center alike. There is indeed no place to hide.

Footnotes: Chapter 14

1. *The EcoSpasm Report,* p. 42.
2. Louis Carabini, "Surviving In An Age Of Uncertainty," *Vital Speeches,* 1975, p. 285. Delivered to the Los Angeles Medical Assoc., Glendale, CA, Jan. 20, 1975.
3. *Ibid.*
4. *Ibid.,* p. 287.
5. John Sims, "U.S. Banks May Be Near Limit On Third World Aid," *Los Angeles Times,* October 3, 1977.
6. *Los Angeles Times,* "IMF Nations Fear New World Economic Slump," September 29, 1977; *Los Angeles Times,* October 1, 1977, "Rich Nations Must Renew."
7. Ceres, "World Economic Disorder," January-February, 1976, pp. 22-3.

8. Brandt, "Working On World Money Gap," *Los Angeles Times,* October 7, 1977; *Newsweek,* September 26, 1977.

9. *Newsweek,* "A Cure For Depression," September 26, 1977.

10. A. Solzhenitsyn, *Warning To The West,* New York: (Farrar, Strauss and Ciroux), 1976.

11. "World Trends and Forecasts," *The Futurist,* February, 1976, pp. 22-3.

8. Brandt, "Working On World Money Gap," *Los Angeles Times,* October 7, 1977; *Newsweek,* September 26, 1977.

9. *Newsweek,* "A Cure For Depression," September 26, 1977.

10. Al Solzhenitsyn, *Warning To The West,* New York: (Farrar, Strauss and Giroux), 1976.

11. "World Trends and Forecasts," *The Futurist,* February, 1977, p. 54-55.

12. *Moody Monthly* magazine, March, 1974.

13. Dostoevsky, *The Brothers Karamazov* (Penguin), p. 763, quoted from Cantelon, *Money Master of the World,* (Logos, 1976), p. 112.

Chapter 15

ECONOMIC CONDITIONS: U.S.A.

"The 1970's have brought the first global double digit inflation on record during peacetime, and the highest unemployment since the Great Depression." The effects are not only general, with special application to the non-affluent countries. The impact is dramatic everywhere, including the U.S.A.

The above statement by Lester Brown, President of Worldwatch Institute, in indicative. Things are not the way they used to be. With the collapse of the Brenton-Woods monetary system, there are louder and louder cries for a new world economic order. However, with worldwide economic troubles stemming from the oil cartel, things are going to get a lot worse before they get better. The U.S. is off the gold standard, and the dollar's purchasing power continues to decline. One overall result is that people are becoming much more concerned about economic security.

Because of inflation, unions continue to strike for higher wages, and that in turn fuels further inflation. In the 1977 East Coast Dock Workers' strike, the workers finally won—and they got over $20,000 a year guaranteed income "whether or not they work." It is staggering, in retrospect. The fact is, we are in a vicious circle. When one commodity, e.g., steel, goes up in price, things made out of steel go up in price. Soon the circle has gone round completely and again we raise the price of steel.

This is currently happening on an accelerating on-going basis worldwide. Increased prices are also due to things like resource scarcity, the law of supply and demand, etc. We constantly find that the demands for higher wages and those other increases inevitably force the cost of production up, so increasing prices again. We all know that when wages rise, prices also must rise, and the dollar must shrink in purchasing power.

Defense costs can be cited as an example. According to the December 12, 1977, *U.S. News and World Report:* "The cost estimates of the major weapons systems being built today have risen by a staggering amount—70 billion dollars over their initial projections. And there is still no end in sight to the phenomenon of U.S. arms costs soaring far beyond the original estimates." Also due to personal and cultural insecurity (meaninglessness, alienation, etc.), people look to material goods to give life satisfaction, and that in turn leads to greed. In the U.S. today, we are demanding more than the system can give. As we demand more—and as politicians offer us more subsidies and government handouts—local, state, and national debt gets deeper and deeper. We tend to listen to those who offer us more, and to ignore those who talk about austerity and tough measures. As humans we are greedy, and we do not always want to face reality.

Inflation is basically an increase in the quantity of money, and it results from people demanding more than they can produce. In 1945 the amount of U.S. currency was $86 billion, whereas today it is $300 billion.[1] A breakdown must come sooner or later.

Once a social system is totally united by products and services, there is an increasing number of "essential" producers—garbagemen, coal miners, dock workers, police, nurses, firemen, air traffic controllers, etc. All of these and many more are coming to realize their new power. As many of their jobs are technologically specialized, workers cannot be easily replaced. When they go on strike, they know they will get at least some of their demands, and that further weakens the economy. The cessation of their services can cripple the country, or at least major parts of it: they wield tremendous power, as shown by the tremendous number of strikes in the last five years. Ten years before that such strikes were relatively rare. It is a new world in which we live, and in the decade ahead the problems will increase—not decrease.

As Schumacher says, we live in a time of misery, not only of poverty: widespread misery is uniquely a phenomenon of our time. In poverty, people keep body and soul together with little to spare. In misery, people do not have even the guarantee of poverty, and the soul in particular suffers. Today cultural-economic-moral vacuums are widespread, and here again the stage is being set for that world leader to step in and to soothe our pains. Schumacher states that misery in both rich and poor nations "is a monstrous and scandalous thing which is altogether abnormal in the history of mankind."[2] The U.S. is certainly not free of misery, as well as some poverty.

FEDERAL DEBT

Another relevant topic involved with the U.S. economy is the Federal debt. More government spending demands more Federal debt. In 1929, the Federal debt was $17 billion. In June, 1976, it was $881 billion. For the last 20 years, government interest payments have risen faster than government revenues. Sooner or later the bank must break.

What is really staggering is that if we take *all* the financial commitments of the government (employee pensions, social security, etc.) it is now *more* than the country's net wealth. Robert Dee, Chairman of the Board of Smithkline Corporation, states:

> When all these financial commitments are projected and all real indebtedness is taken into

account, the federal debt right now is over $6 trillion.[3]

John W. Kendrich of George Washington University has calculated the entire net wealth of the American people at $5.7 trillion.[4] Thus in 50 years the Federal debt has gone from *$17 billion to $6,000 billion dollars,* and now as a nation the U.S. would be unable to make all payments if they were due. Note the following comparisons:[5]

	Trade Deficit	National Budget	Years for 100 Billion Increase	Value of the $
1962	None	100 billion	300	1.00
1971	None	200 billion	9	.82
1975/6	9.3 Bil.	300 billion	4	.62
1977	30 Bil.	400 billion	2	.53

These figures, along with the fact that, according to Associated Press, almost half of the nation's 215 million people receive a significant portion of their income from some agency of Government, lead to some unsettling conclusions.

Robert F. Dee puts the situation clearly in "The Greatest Danger to Be Feared" in *Vital Speeches of the Day* of December 15, 1976. He regards these statistics on government subsidies, employment, and spending as signposts. He suggests that taken singly each of these raise the point of alarm, but when taken together they can point in only one direction—total control of the American people by the government. He suggests that history has shown over and over again that freedom goes as government grows.

In that same journal, Howard Kershner, visiting Professor of Current Economic Problems at the Northwood Institute, suggests that borrowing money to create jobs leads to difficulties, increased debt, and though there is a greater quantity of money there is a steady decline in the value of the dollar. When there is an inflationary boom that is kept going by increasing the quantity of money, he argues, there is a false prosperity. However, he warns that in country after country the value of the unit of exchange can approach zero, and, as that happens, to increase the quantity of money will no longer have any effect. He warns that if that point is reached the options are to return to freedom, sadder and wiser, yet with most of the country's wealth gone, or to head into the totalitarian state. He suggests that this latter course is likely to take place unless immediate remedial action is taken in the near future.[16]

Kershner goes on to give examples of countries devaluing—Brazil, Argentina, Uruguay, Peru, France, Italy, Portugal—they have all seriously devalued and Kershner suggests that there is no reason why the same will not happen in the United States. He urges that it should be recognized that "we are going down that road at an ever increasing speed."

At the risk of being repetitious, let us emphasize some things in that statement by Howard Kershner. Other countries have already gone down the path being followed by the U.S., and increasing the quantity of money has not solved their problems. The real threat (by Western standards) of a totalitarian state is very much over our heads. Our economic thrust is at an ever-increasing rate downhill, and the decline of the dollar is a very serious and present fact of life. The economic problems facing us are surely too real to be ignored.

Kershner refers to the useless attempts of wage and price control, and to the current loss in value of other currencies around the world. He further states that this has happened many times and is happening even now in the United States where the dollar has lost three-quarters of its value. He urges that action to stop this decline must be implemented, for otherwise the remaining quarter will be lost far more rapidly than the first three-quarters. To stop the rot, sacrifice and hardship would be called for, but this would be mild compared with future suffering if the present trend of inflation is continued until the dollar is completely destroyed. Such a prospect is there, in the immediate future, and it cannot be avoided without some sacrifice, so the sooner it is tackled the lower the penalty will be. Conversely, the longer it is put off the greater the suffering, the loss of freedom, of the free market system of economics, and a free government.

Kershner suggests a return to the gold standard and makes the point that no nation on the gold standard has ever suffered a serious inflation, whereas no nation that has left the gold standard has ever avoided such inflation.

He further urges action, because no nation that has proceeded as far with inflation as the U.S. at present has ever avoided ruining its monetary unit. The only way to be the first to do so is to face the facts and to take action before it is too late.

Kershner in another article, "Why Civilizations Rise and Fall," makes the point that civilizations have flourished on the basis of trusted money, money that did not progressively lose its value and money for which people were willing to work long and hard and also to save with confidence.[7] He argues that this will lead to capital accumulation which is necessary for the financing of research, science, art, music, and culture of all kinds.

He argues that, conversely, if people do not trust the stability of the purchasing power of their monetary unit, an irresistible demand for higher wages sets in and prices follow in proportion. He reminds us that labor costs at least 90 percent of the ultimate price and that there is no such thing as controlling prices for long unless wages also are controlled. He elaborates by showing that both of these are impossible, for attempts at price and wage control always result in two things: the black market and scarcity of products.

Kershner adds a touching personal note:

> I have carried my investigations into some sixty countries throughout the world. I have been in the middle of several inflations, and I see a close and clear resemblance between what is going on

in our country and what has taken place in other countries.[8]

He notes that 42 years is said to be the longest time any monetary unit has held on to any considerable part of its purchasing power after it ceased to be convertible to silver or gold on demand. The U.S. has been off the gold standard 42 years as of 1978. That is a thought-provoking fact of life.

It is instructive for us to look at what happened to Germany about 1923. Inflation was so extreme that in January, 1919, nine marks would buy $1. Less than five years later, in November, 1923, it took 4,200,000,000,000 (4 trillion) marks to buy $1. A newspaper that cost 6,000 marks at 7 a.m. cost up to 130,000 marks for the evening edition.

Alvin Toffler, in *The Eco-Spasm Report,* states:

> If pressures like these were suddenly to build up within today's superannuated industrial nations, we would witness the breakdown of the integrated money system.[9]

SOUND MONEY, MORAL ADVANCE, AND PROSPERITY ARE LINKED

Kershner states:

> Throughout history periods of sound money have been marked by moral advance and prosperity. Conversely, periods of unsound money have been accompanied by moral decline and economic hard times . . . . Sound money has been at the basis of every civilization that has developed, and when it is deserted and worthless paper is substituted for it, that marks the beginning of decline.[10]

Sound money . . . moral advance . . . and prosperity

are linked. It has long been recognized that the moral decay of a civilization soon led to its overthrow. Sir Leonard Woolley excavated at Ur, and he found a culture that flourished even earlier than Abraham's day. The recovered tablets showed that moral decay was setting in, and soon the prior greatness of Ur was only a memory. The history of Rome illustrates the same principle—and there are many such examples.

The Decade of Shock will soon be on us, and its birth pains must lead to a delivery, whether alive or dead. Our moral judgments are highly relevant—and the decisions of today might well be deciding whether we are to produce a monster or a suckling baby that can yet be nurtured and so survive even that potentially disastrous period.

Footnotes: Chapter 15

1. Howard Kershner, *Vital Speeches,* "Stop Inflation And Depression Now," October 15, 1975, p. 12.
2. "Small Is Still Beautiful," *The Futurist,* April, 1977, p. 97.
3. Robert F. Dee, "The Greatest Danger To Be Feared?", *Vital Speeches Of The Day,* December 15, 1976.
4. *Ibid.*
5. *Ibid.*
6. *Vital Speeches,* October 15, 1975.
7. *Vital Speeches,* January 15, 1974.
8. *Ibid.*
9. Toffler, *The Eco-Spasm Report,* p. 40.
10. *Vital Speeches,* Jan. 15, 1974.

Chapter 16

WATCH OUT —
THE COMPUTER'S
AFTER YOU!

The last Book of the Bible contains many pictures, and some of them seem to describe conditions that begin to face us. Perhaps its visionary setting has a factual fulfillment just around the corner.

"NO ONE CAN BUY OR SELL
UNLESS . . . "

One of its statements concerning the end time is that "No man might buy or sell, save he that had the mark, or the name of the beast, or the number of his name" (Revelation 13:17).

A generation ago such a statement was mainly of interest only to the students of Bible prophecy as such, but today it can be seen as a pointer to a situation that is almost on us. Coming events are casting ominous shadows.

TRW is Cleveland's automotive-aerospace multi-company, and a report by Dane L. Thomas in *Barron's* of September 20, 1976, illustrates the point. He elaborates the fact that TRW, the $2.5 billion maker of auto parts and electronic systems, had taken a giant step forward in the Electronic Funds Transfer (EFT) business when it recently announced that it had acquired Singer Company's inventory and service contracts in North America.

Something of the relevance of this to the so-called "mark of the beast" of Revelation can be seen as Thomas elaborates some of the implications of that deal. It points up the struggle to obtain stakes in the growing EFT business which could eventually eliminate many functions of banks and lead to vast changes in the financial structure of the U.S. One of the prime forces in the move was the Federal Reserve System because it wanted to cut down on paperwork. With that in mind it has supervised the installation of houses where checkless transactions are processed via computers.

As the article further points out, many of the older generation are reluctant to give up their traditional use of checks, and the smaller rural banks are setting up "legal roadblocks". They want to stop the inroads into their business by the large commercial banks with their computerized systems.

A TREND THAT IS "IRREVERSIBLE"

That particular article makes many statements that are far-reaching in their implications, and similar statements could be multiplied from other authorities. One of the points made is that "the basic trend to EFT, in the opinion of most experts, is irreversible." We might see dangers, as those smaller rural banks do, and we might recognize that we are heading to a faceless community controlled by a master computer, but we cannot reverse the process. It is, indeed, irreversible. The trend toward the electronic transfer of funds is gathering speed alarmingly.

OLDER PEOPLE HESITATE

Although surveys show that most younger people are receptive to EFT systems, many older ones hesitate to surrender their tangible evidence of money, such as bank savings passbooks and checks.

Another objection of consumers is that EFT systems, by instantaneously recording transactions, can eliminate the check "float" upon which many individuals and corporations rely for the several days of grace they now have when they write a check.

Of concern, too, is the growing possibility of computer error or outright fraud. To eliminate this, suppliers are researching techniques for applying increasing safeguards. Addressograph-Multigraph, for example, has introduced a device to protect the magnetic strip process for encoding information on credit-debit cards. The device is to ensure that the cards cannot be tampered with by outsiders.

Coming events have been casting their shadows for years. Before there can be a birth, there must first be a conception. The conception of the ideas about electronic transfer of funds has been around for years now. *Business Week* of January 13, 1968, had a special report headed *"Money Goes Electronic—In the 1970's."* As it rightly stated in the introductory remarks, "The change will do much more than speed banking; it will drastically alter cherished habits of business and society."

It further states, "A single identification card will replace cash in all but a few minor transactions." One card? It brings us very close to the "mark of the beast" we talked about at the beginning of this chapter. That ancient Bible writer displayed more than remarkably incisive forethought: the theologians call it predictive prophecy, inspired by the Holy Spirit of God.

THE COMPUTER AS AN OMNIPRESENT, INDISPENSABLE "THIRD MAN"

Banks on a collision course with other industries . . . public and political outcries over computerized credit ratings and the encroachment on individual rights . . . hookups that embrace virtually all financial transactions across the nation—these are all envisaged in that *Business Week* article. Part of the report was as follows:

> On this concept, visionary bankers and computer experts want to build a nationwide electronic network of instantaneous bookkeeping and financial services that would be connected with everybody, much as the telephone network is

now. The computer would become an omnipresent, indispensable "third man" in the exchange of money.

Omnipresent and indispensable: that is strong language, the sort of language theologians use for Almighty God. The tentacles of a mindless controlling force are attempting to take over from Almighty God Who made man in His own image. The computer is set to destroy man's personality while so logically offering him ease of function and financial security. The birth pains of the Decade of Shock are about to commence. It looks horribly probable that a monster will be born in that Decade of Shock.

VISION OF 1984

The article actually has a subheading, "Vision of 1984." Here is part of the argument at that point:

What, for instance, should go into an accurate measure of a man's financial responsibility: How much he drinks? Who is to have access to the data? Will a person be alerted whenever someone examines his file? Will he be told who is investigating him? What recourse will he have if there is an error in the system?

The article goes on to discuss the envisaged problems, and the terminology is revealing: "The danger is not so much of evil, but of miscalculation." — "The credit card scene is now a nightmare." — "Either cataclysmic shakeouts or considerable compromise between the multidimensional rivalries must come if the checkless society is to follow." — "Banks are now bidding to become . . . 'the octopi of finance'."

It is relevant to ask, "Where does it all end? Is all this a preshadowing of that coming 'mark of the beast'?"

As long ago as December 29, 1969, the L. A. Times forecast the possibility of such a checkless society. Arelo Sederberg wrote at that time, "By the late 1970's or early '80's, money could become an electronic impulse. Bankers long have discussed a 'checkless' or 'moneyless' society, and recently one farsighted industrialist, Simon Ramo, Chairman of the Executive Committee of TRW Inc., forecast the advent of electronic money within our lifetime." [1]

"By the late 1970's or early '80's." He was right. Here we are at the end of the '70's. Sederberg quotes Louis B. Lundberg, then Chairman of the Bank of America, as stating that all the technology for a checkless or even cashless society is at hand now, and that it is largely market forces that would determine the speed at which we would move.

Almost a decade has passed since that was written, and the momentum has gathered pace quickly. Thus the UNIS Corporation of California advertised in *TV Guide* of October 5, 1972:

In the beginning . . . there were cash, checks, and plastic credit cards . . . and it was good.

Now:

Electric Money hath come.

The advent of Electric Money marks the coming of a new era in the monetary system . . . The beginning of the end of cash, checks, and plastic credit cards . . . Change that will affect everyone.

You have a unique opportunity to be among the first to learn of and about Electric Money and to obtain an Electric Money Card.

(An address is given for further information.)

AN INSIDIOUS TAKEOVER

By 1975, the takeover was nearer to completion, and the August 4, 1975, *Business Week* had an article in its finance section, *"Bank Cards Take Over The Country."* It makes the point that the takeover by electronic banking is faster than any but the most optimistic could have thought possible. One result is to change dramatically the banking and savings habits of millions of Americans. The article suggests that eventually electronic banking will revolutionize the concept of money itself and probably will force profound changes in how the Federal Reserve regulates the money supply of the nation. It will touch off competition for the nation's financial business, different from anything ever known before.

The mechanics are so easy that Mr. Private Citizen will be captured in a net with ramifications that are frightening and even monstrous. He will have a magnetically encoded plastic card that is similar to the present Visa Card or Master Charge. He will now be able to deposit or withdraw cash and to transfer money between different types of accounts without writing checks — and without setting his feet inside conventional banking offices. The card will be popped into a computer terminal in a center such as a retail store or even a factory cafeteria.

This is bypassing legal problems about opening branches of banks, for those restrictive rules do not apply to the installing of terminals. A bank owning the parent computer might be around the corner, or it might be thousands of miles away in another State. The first National Bank in New York has about 300 branches in that State, and that is the only State in which it can operate its branches. However, that same *Business Week* article reported that the Bank already had 3,000 check-guarantee terminals, some of them out of New York State in New Jersey.

It tells of a survey by consultants Booz-Allen and Hamilton showing it is anticipated that by 1983 electronic banking will eliminate 14% of the checks that might otherwise have been written, and that 11 billion transactions a year would be handled electronically instead of by cash.

DRASTIC CHANGES AHEAD

Merchant-operated terminals are springing up all over the U.S., and even in 1975 it could be written of a State such as Nebraska that "a First Federal electronic terminal is within reach of 50% of the State's population."

Banking authority, Paul S. Nadler of Rutgers University, is quoted in that same article as stating that this spread of terminals is going to be statewide and nationwide, and that the local monopoly will die. Our electronic masters will bring drastic changes to our whole way of life in the Decade of Shock.

For whether we like it or not, you and I are involved. When we accepted that first credit card we gave our tacit consent to the process. We agreed, maybe reluctantly or even unknowingly, to the concept of the banks and the merchants combining so that they could begin tying the hands of us the customers, behind our backs. Between 1972 and 1975 more than 20 clearing houses were established around the United States, processing over one million electronic transactions each month, and with the potential to serve 90% of the United States.

Hundreds of companies and local government agencies pay their workers by automatic bank transfers, with checks not involved, and even bills are met without the traditional signing of a check. Over four million Americans have their Social Security payments deposited straight to their banking accounts.

By the time we enter the 1980's, according to the *Barron's* article mentioned above, it is expected that 18 million Americans will be actively using this service.

Many of us have walked into banks and have been invited to see a demonstration of the automated teller and cash-dispensing machines. By the end of 1975 there were 4,000 of these in the U.S., installed by 1,300 financial institutions. By the end of 1976 the trend had increased so that nearly 20% of banks were using automated tellers.

"INNOCENT INNOVATIONS"

There are other "innocent innovations." Tens of thousands of retail stores and service outlets have installed electronic point-of-sales terminals, basically for the purposes of credit and check verification. It would only need the "go-ahead" from management for this to be converted into full EFT systems. Thus your simple supermarket transactions are another link in that chain of controlling you financially when the time is ripe.

Major retail concerns are deeply involved in these coming events that are casting their ominous shadows. Sears, Montgomery Ward, and J.C. Penney, have been busy installing terminals that are hooked into computers, with the idea of having their own EFT operations. Master Charge and Visa are deeply involved in the standardization of debit cards to trigger the withdrawal and deposit of funds, and many other commercial giants are now much more than stirring into wakeful consciousness of the prizes for the grasping. Suppliers of equipment are competing for huge contracts in such areas as the automated teller market and customer-inquiring terminals.

Another giant is NCR, reported to be installing its equipment in 75-90 supermarkets a month. Its major competition in the supermarket field is National Semi-Conductor, with reported current doubling of its point-of-sales hardware volume each year.

A new factor is the entrance into the market of IBM, with computer-based-terminals available on a leasing arrangement, rather than being outright sales, as has been the more usual practice with EFT hardware. That company is also competing strenuously for smaller retail stores with low-cost hardware: restaurants and similar businesses are fast becoming involved. IBM has even entered the field of "Cash-flow" cards for transferring funds, paying taxes, and various other functions traditionally associated only with banks.

The traumas associated with our approach to the coming decade are by no means imaginary. It is all too true that you, the individual, the private citizen, are very much involved. The fact is, the birth pains have started. When the time is full and "maturity" is reached, our whole way of life will be changed.

COMPUTER ERRORS ARE POSSIBLE . . .
BUT BIG BROTHER IS WATCHING

Needless to say, there are other dangers. Not the least of which is a computer error, for the computer ultimately depends on a human who feeds it information. That error could cause you untold damage, starting with the refusal of funds or the canceling of a good credit rating, and leading down to the everyday activities of your life. You might be surprised at the way a computer read-out could affect your hairdresser's attitude toward you, or that of the girl on the checkout point at the supermarket.

Big Brother is watching you. You'd better believe it. That computer's right behind you.

Outright fraud is yet another possibility, and researchers are doing their utmost to eliminate known possibilities such as that of tampering with cards by "outsiders."

The processes that have been more or less greatly accepted in the 1970's have opened the door to a checkless society in the 1980's. That same article in *Barron's* puts it this way: "The widespread boom of credit cards has supplanted checks in many functions, and this in itself, says EFT proponents, is a major step toward a totally checkless society."

Some will shrug these things off, maybe with a casual remark such as, "We're in the computer age. We can't stop progress." That, of course, is true. Computers touch our lives in all sorts of expected and unexpected ways, not only in the commercial world but with scientific and academic research, traffic control, plane reservations, and even medical diagnoses.

The computer will give us in seconds what might otherwise take years to assess. None of us can compete as individuals, yet ultimately the computer itself is controlled by individuals. Alphonse Chapanis of Johns Hopkins University puts it well in his study, *"Interactive Human Communication:"*

> Most computers still require an intermediary between the ultimate user and the computer, someone who is familiar with the way the computer works and with the special language that is needed to address it.

Who will ultimately control the master computer? Who will be that "intermediary?" The devilish possibilities are frightening, with a veritable Antichrist at the helm at some time soon.

Footnotes: Chapter 16

1. Arelo Sederberg, "A Moneyless Society? It's Just Possible." *Los Angeles Times,* (Dec. 29, 1969).

Chapter 17

THE COMMON MARKET

Students of Bible prophecy have long declared that in a coming day there will be a revived Roman Empire. In earlier years it was common to point to the Roman Catholic Church and to argue that here was that Empire.

THE REVIVED ROMAN EMPIRE?

In recent years it has been more common to link the emerging European Common Market with that revived Roman Empire and to look for an eventual combination of ten nations being involved. This is in part based on a dream by the Babylonian King Nebuchadnezzar about a giant figure. The dream was interpreted by the prophet Daniel (Chapter 2). The figure had ten toes which were a mixture of iron and clay. Daniel told the king that the figure spoke of a series of future kingdoms. The last ones were ten kings having a mixture of iron (strength) and clay (weakness).

Stephen Mulligan in *The European Community,* of September-October, 1977, points out that it was The Treaty of Rome that founded the European Economic Community. Obviously that is an interesting connection with Rome.

One fact is clear. Experts who know nothing of Bible prophecy are speaking as if they had spent a fair amount of time studying it. Their analyses of world conditions show the stage is being set in space-time history for the fulfillment of Biblical prophecy. The ancient prophets portrayal of a new world order, revived Roman Empire, and a last days religious world dictator (who will demand to be worshipped as God), are even "prophesied" by the secular writers. In *The Toynbee-Ikeda Dialogue* (1976, p. 243), Daisaku Ikeda sums up eminent historian Arnold Toynbee's recent views and offers his own comments:

> Regarding the process of world unification under a single government, you make several points, which I might summarize as follows. China is likely to play a leading role in this unification. The Chinese principle of rule will serve as an inspiring example. A dictator with outstanding leadership ability may be a necessity in the course of world unification. You expect to see the rise of a new world religion that will serve as a catalyst for the spiritual unity of all nations . . . . I feel that a precedent for future world unity may be found in the current European attempt to achieve an intracontinental federation of nations . . . . To be sure, we need an integral system of religion or philosophy that will help to incorporate all nations into one body. The achievement of this religious or spiritual unity may require a personality capable of effective leadership.

Robert Paine, in a 1973 interview with Dick Spangler (KGIL Radio, San Fernando, California), stated his belief that "all over the world"—in Africa, Asia, large sections of Europe, and in the U.S.—there was the possibility of "one man taking over the whole thing and ruling simply by command." Paine is an authority on dictators, having written definitive volumes on Hitler, Mao Tse Tung, Ho Chi Minh, and others. Solzhenitsyn, in his *Warning to the West* (1976, p. 79), states: "We are approaching a major turning point in world history, in the history of civilization. It has already been noted by specialists in various areas." Alvin Toffler, author of *Future Shock* states in his *The Eco-Spasm Report* (1975, p. 74-75; 3):

> The nation-state can no longer cope with the basic problems posed by the shift toward super-industrialism. In economic terms, the nation-state is a product of the industrial revolution and, as such, has served its purpose. In the technically advanced countries (if not in the developing areas) it is now fundamentally obsolete. It will not disappear, but it will shrink in power. Indeed it already has. If the eco-spasm analysis does anything, it reveals the pitiful, bumbling incapacity of national governments and their politicians to deal with new economic forces that transcend national boundaries.

He also says:

> What is happening, no more, no less, is the breakdown of industrial civilization on the planet and the first fragmentary appearance of a wholly new and dramatically different social order: a super-industrial civilization that will be technological, but no longer industrial.

What are the facts, and are these the ten kingdoms that Daniel talked about? In *The Atlantic Community Quarterly* of Spring, 1976, there is an article entitled "The Eurogroup." The opening two paragraphs are relevant:

> The Eurogroup is a grouping of Defense Ministers of European member governments within the NATO framework. It is open to all European members of NATO. Those taking part at

> present are Belgium, Denmark, Germany, Greece, Italy, Luxembourg, the Netherlands, Norway, Turkey, and the United Kingdom.
>
> The basic aim of the Eurogroup can be simply stated: it is to help to ensure a stronger and more cohesive European contribution to the common defense, and thus to strengthen the Alliance and the security in which its peoples live.

We count them, and we find that ten nations are involved. Strictly speaking, Greece was not formally included at that time, but her inclusion was well under way.

Daniel's mixture of iron and clay might very well be taking place before your eyes. Economic and monetary problems have added to the problems of man, and these are surely areas of "clay." Even within the ten countries listed above there are enormous differences in such areas as inflation and economic growth. "Iron and Clay" is a fitting description.

This leads to another important aspect of strength and weakness in this association of strong and weak nations, for ideally this grouping is supposed to make possible the best use of defense resources. It is also intended to provide a forum for the harmonizing of political and strategic questions that infringe on the interest of each member of the group.

MILLIONS OF DOLLARS LOST
THROUGH DUPLICATION

Elsewhere in this volume we have elaborated the huge problems facing the NATO Defense Alliance because of duplication, leading to billions of dollars of waste. It is easy to talk of the intention to "ensure a stronger and more cohesive European contribution to the common defense," but it is a quite different matter to see it put into effect.

The same report tells us that "another important objective of the Eurogroup is to encourage and give support to the continuing and vital presence in Europe of American and Canadian forces." These are basically English-speaking people, with Canada a member of the Commonwealth which traditionally is headed up by the United Kingdom. Historically, the U.S. has strong political and racial affinities with the U.K. as well as with the European nations.

The U.S. and NATO certainly add some iron to a federation that otherwise would be very much (though not exclusively) a component of clay. The article to which we have referred points out that the military power of the United States and the clear recognition of basic interests has led successive U.S. Administrations to commit themselves and to deploy their power to help deter external attack at any point in the area of the Alliance. This remains the linchpin of Western defense and it is crucial to NATO's continued success in being able to maintain the security of its peoples in the face of the formidable military capacity of the Warsaw Pact peoples.

Undoubtedly the U.S. and Canadian forces are an essential part of the European grouping. The above report elaborates by quoting from the "Declaration on Atlantic Relations," signed by heads of NATO governments in Brussels on June 26, 1974:

> All members of the Alliance agree that the continued presence of Canadian and substantial U.S. forces in Europe plays an irreplaceable role in the defense of North America as well as of Europe. Similarly, the substantial forces of the European allies serve to defend Europe and North America as well.

FACTORS UNITING AND DIVIDING

Some progress has been made "by the gradual harmonization of tactical concepts and doctrines now being achieved by the Eurogroup countries," as the above report puts it. Collaboration is being extended in various fields, such as in tactical communications systems, compatibility of logistics, basic tactical concepts and doctrines, military medical functions, multilateral training arrangements, and centralized training of such groups as jet pilots and operators of surface to surface missiles.

The road ahead is certainly not easy, but positive steps are being taken along lines outlined above, and in other ways. The position was put well by Belgium's Prime Minister, Leo Tindemans, in a report, "European Union," dated December 29, 1975, to the members of the European Council:

> The aim of European Union should be to overcome the age-old conflicts which are often artificially maintained between Nation-States, to build a more human society in which, along with mutual respect for our national and cultural origins, the accent will be placed more on the factors uniting us than on those dividing us . . . .

Factors uniting—and factors dividing—it looks remarkably like Daniel's statement about a mixture of iron and clay. Tindemans urged the need for an authoritative parliament for the European Union countries, democratically elected, with a real increase in power. There also should be, he urged, real powers available to the European Council. "The institutional structures set up by the Treaties have shown themselves in practice to be too weak to give the necessary continuing political momentum needed for the construction of Europe."

THE POLITICAL UNION OF EUROPE?

It has been agreed that elections will decide the personnel of the 410 members of the European Parliament, "and some observers view it as a fore-runner of the political union of Europe," according to Don Cook in *The Los Angeles Times,* July 13, 1976. Its practical efforts at cooperation remain very much a matter of conjecture.

As Cook points out, "It is still unable even to agree on a common daylight saving time system for Europe next summer."

The areas of negotiated agreement between the ten member countries are extensive, e.g., prices for Mediterranean foods being traded, qualities set for traded fruit and vegetables, and even specifics of wine measuring. Some of these are elaborated in *European Community* of September-October, 1977, and it becomes clear that the chances of agreement are decreased greatly as any one new member is admitted. As that report makes clear, the entry of any one new member automatically reduces the arithmetical chances of agreement in a system where most of the decisions must necessarily be unanimous. Obviously this means that enlargement could mean that decisions and policies would be harder to reach.

THE TEN NATIONS AND POLITICAL CHANGE

If the European Common Mart is part of Daniel's ten nations, the number is likely to so remain for a considerable time—or until God ordains otherwise. Time will tell.

Free intermigration is a necessary part of the grouping, and it is likely that the number will remain stable at ten. Although there has been debate over Greece's affiliation for membership, there has been a readiness to accept her ahead of the willingness expressed toward Spain and Portugal. Both of these nations have made overtures to "join the club," but each has high hurdles to clear. Portugal's weak economy is a hindrance to full participation, and until recently Spain posed a political problem with its traditional Arab world links. It is more anti-Israel than some of the other nations, but various pressures, including the threat of oil embargoes, tend to change this.

Political changes take place overnight, and that can be illustrated in this very matter of relationships with and attitudes toward the Arab states. The *Los Angeles Times* of October 30, 1977, reported: "The European Common Market Saturday bowed to Arab economic pressure and signed a joint statement supporting a Palestinian homeland

and condemning Israeli occupation of Arab lands.''

Undoubtedly this was a major political victory for the Arabs, for it meant that the Common Market countries were going beyond the economic and trade matters to which they had agreed to restrict themselves. They stopped short of total complicity with the arms and economic embargo demanded by the Arabs, with a full recognition of the Palestine Liberation Organization. However, the individual countries did vote in the United Nations meeting of the same week, condemning Israel for establishing settlements in territories formerly occupied by the Arabs.

Anthony Crosland, President of the Council of Ministries of the European Community who made this report, went on to say that ''the essential basis for economic integration is therefore wholly lacking.'' That is so with countries already admitted to the club. Some knocking at the door present even greater problems.

Constantine Karamanlis is on record as stating:

> Greece has officially declared several times, and repeated on April 5, 1977, that it is ready to accept all existing Community legislation. Far from hindering procedural development that will reinforce European cohesion, Greece intends to contribute to it by promoting the great ideal of the Community's founders to realize the gradual and decisive unification of Europe.

Karamanlis went on to point to 15 years of cooperation on the part of Greece, and further stated:

> The Hellenic Government is convinced that its own political will, as well as that of the nine EC member states, has been secured and has been solemnly manifested many times—that all the problems to come will find, within a relatively brief period, solutions favorable to both sides in conformity with the spirit and the letter

of the Treaty of Rome and the other Community treaties.[1]

We (Weldon and Wilson) would not be surprised to see some variations in the individual nations making up the Common Market Community, but it is at least interesting to see this number of ten being discussed so often. Possibly there is at least some relationship to those ten kingdoms of Nebuchadnezzar's dream as interpreted by Daniel.

A "FOR-EVER" KINGDOM?

If this is true, there is something even more important. That same interpretation by Daniel said that not only would the iron and the clay not mix together, but also "in the days of these kings shall the God of heaven set up a kingdom, which shall never be destroyed—it shall break in pieces and consume all these kingdoms, and it shall stand for ever" (Daniel 2:44).

That would suggest divine intervention at the time of the ten kingdoms. Other prophecies (e.g. Daniel Chapter 7) have been written about at great length, with the various symbols (such as a lion, an eagle, and a bear) interpreted as referring to the superpowers of today. Time will tell. Certain it is that the Decade of Shock will bring many answers, possibly including an understanding of Daniel's prophecies.

Footnotes: Chapter 17

1. Stephen Milligan, "The Nine Ponder Enlargement," *European Community,* September-October, 1977, p. 9.

Chapter 18

SO WHY BOTHER?!

The previous chapters have been shocking. The possibility does exist that man might substantially destroy himself in the near future. Historian John C. Green has said, "The events of the twentieth century bear tragic witness to the realism of the biblical portrait of man."[1] This portrait states that man is noble—created in God's own image—but also that he is fallen. He is in rebellion against his Creator. This has affected him spiritually, psychologically, and socially. Man is noble and at the same time cruel. Acts of heroism and compassion reign equally with acts of greed and terror. Unfortunately, our world is now united by so many complex factors, each of us must collectively partake in the world's future.

Our purpose in writing this book is not to cause unyielding despair—an outlook of hopeless pessimism. There is hope. While we are very concerned about our immediate future, we are ultimately optimists. We do not intend to say, "Well, that's it folks, there is no hope," and leave it there. Ideas have consequences, and cultural pessimism about the future breeds social decay and heightens immorality. "If the future is hopeless, why not live it up now?" is the kind of attitude that can destroy the future today. Many people have adopted such a view, and we see the effects all around us in the resurgence of cultural hedonism. There is a large number of young people who are, in the deepest meaning of the term, lost. They wander between meaninglessness, escapism, and violence trying to make some sense out of both the fact of their existence and the uncertainty of whether or not there will be a future. There will be . . . and it can be a future far beyond all comparison if we make the right decision. In this chapter we will tell you how.

The reasons for our current social disintegration are numerous. The new narcissism of the many human potential, "man-is-God" movements (Erhard Seminars Training [est], the eastern gurus, Scientology, Transcendental Meditation*, etc.); the immorality, greed, social anarchy or apathy, and personal destruction so easily fostered by involvement in the occult and eastern religions; the degradation of sexual standards; the increasing disrespect for law, authority, and people; are all part of the reason for our cultural demise.

The intent of this book is twofold. First, to assess the condition of the world realistically: fantasy and escapism solve nothing. We have only partially touched upon this herein. Second, we intend to show how we can accept reality and also have hope, how we may realistically assess our condition and simultaneously be optimistic. We have pointed out some of the problems, and we intend to provide some constructive steps that can help, as well as the ultimate solution.

CULTURAL DESPAIR

Today, unfortunately, many people—scholars and those most knowledgeable, as well—are pessimistic. We might list a few examples of the many we have collected that are indicative. Norman O'Brown says, "Today, even the survival of humanity is a utopian hope."[2] Scientist Ralph

---

*See John Weldon's book on this for an exposé of its true purpose, Hindu nature, and dangers of suicide and insanity.

Lapp says, "No one, not even the most brilliant scientist alive today, really knows where science is taking us. We are aboard a train which is gathering speed, racing down a track on which there are an unknown number of switches leading to unknown destinations. No single scientist is in the engine cab, and there may be demons at the switch. Most of society is in the caboose looking backward."[3] Nobel prize winner George Wald, stated, "I think the people who see the situation objectively are horrified at the prospects for human survival on this planet."[4] Dr. Francis Schaeffer shares this thought: "The men who really understand are terrorized."[5] Popular novelist Kurt Vonnegut believes, "Things are going to get worse and worse and never get better again."[6] As we have said, our purpose in writing this book is not to leave readers with no hope. Rather we intend, through a realistic assessment of our condition, to point them to a higher reality. This reality is that ultimate solution of which we spoke, and it is deeply personal—which is where the solution to any problem lies. Modern man generally feels there is no ultimate purpose or absolute truth in life. This is a result of how he views his existence. The Proverbs state, "as a man thinks in his heart, so is he."

EVOLUTIONARY ADVANCEMENT

One of the main reasons for man's existential despair is the theory of evolution. Darwin removed the idea of God as Creator, and when God "died," man died soon after. When pressed to its logical conclusion, evolution states man has no ultimate purpose and is reduced to that which created him—the impersonal elements of time + matter + chance. Few people are aware of how destructive the consequences of evolutionary thinking have been. This is especially tragic when we consider the fact that there is no real hard evidence for evolution. Such a statement will sound incredulous to some, but both authors (Wilson and Weldon) were at one time evolutionists. However, along with thousands of scientists in Europe and America, we rejected evolution by thorough examination of the evidence against it. As an example we could cite the 1200 page research of the well known Swedish Botanist, Dr. Nils H. Nilsson, who spent 40 years trying to prove evolution. In his *Synthetische Artbildung* he says, "The crises of the theory of evolution is complete . . . . The idea of evolution rests on pure belief . . . . Has there really been an evolution? Are the proofs of its occurrence tenable? After a detailed and comprehensive review of the facts, we have been forced to give the answer. No!"[7] How we view our origins tends to affect how we view our lives. If we believe we were created by a just and loving God who will hold us accountable for our actions and judge us after death (Hebrews 9:27: "It is given for every man to die once, and then comes judgment."), we will reflect this as we live out our daily lives. If we believe we came into being by chance, exist for awhile, and then die forever—with no one to answer to—this will also influence our lives.

There are many questions we could touch on here—why most scientists accept evolution when there is no evidence for it, how it influenced Marx, Stalin, and Hitler, the ways in which it has laid waste our culture, and how it has destroyed faith in God and the Bible for millions of people, but the interested reader will have to pursue this on his own. The better volumes are Dr. J. F. Coppedge's *Evolution: Possible or Impossible?,* Dr. R. L. Wysong's *The Creation-Evolution Controversy,* Dr. A. E. Wilder-Smith's *Man's Origin—Man's Destiny,* Dr. Henry M. Morris' *The Troubled Waters of Evolution,* Dr. Bolton Davidheiser's *Evolution and the Christian Faith,* Dr. R. E. D. Clark's *Darwin: Before and After,* Dr. Marshall Hall's *The Truth: God or Evolution,* and others. Needless to say an unbiased examination of the data point more toward special creation than evolution.

WHAT IS TRUTH?

Two thousand years ago a prisoner about to be crucified told Pilate that his kingdom was not of this world, and went on to state: "You say correctly that I am a king. For this I have been born and for this I have come into the world, to bear witness of the truth. Every one who is of the truth hears My voice" (John 18:37). Pilate queried, *"What is truth?"*—which has become the perennial question. Is it possible to know truth—absolute, ultimate truth? We believe so and will present our reasons in this chapter. An unbiased examination of the evidence for the legitimacy of Christ's claims on men, no matter how rigorous the study, leaves no other conclusion. In this book we have discussed some of the issues of this life, but what about the issues of the next life—if indeed there is one?

DEATH AND THE MEANING OF MAN

If the world were to solve all its problems tomorrow, it would only postpone the inevitable. In a world of uncertainties the one final reality is death. If a man dies, will he live again, or will he be annihilated? The evolutionary humanist (or materialist) view says when we die, that's it forever. As we have said, such a view has consequences. We can see these by examining the statements of modern prophets, philosophers, and scholars. These involve a meaningless existence now and eternal nothingness then. Sartre said, "Man is absurd, but he must grimly act as if he were not;"[8] and "Man is a useless passion."[9] Albert Camu said, "I proclaim that I believe in nothing and that everything is absurd."[10] Timothy Leary: " . . . all human purposes, including your own, are solemn self-deceptions."[11] Kierkegaard stated that, "The purpose of life is to be brought to the highest degree of disgust with life."[12]

Commenting on his six-hour film showing a man sleeping, Andy Warhol stated, "It keeps you from thinking. I wish I were a machine."[13] Dostoyevsky said, "Gentlemen, I am tormented by questions; answer them for me;"[14] and historian Arnold Toynbee says that, "Our present form of society is truly repulsive . . . . The formidable fundamental question now is: 'What is life for?' "[15] H. L. Mencken refers to the cosmos as: " . . . a gigantic flywheel making 10,000 revolutions a minute. Man is a sick fly taking a dizzy ride on it. The basic fact about human experience is not that it is a tragedy, but that it is a bore. It is not that it is predominantly painful, but that it is lacking in any sense.''[16] Philosopher Bertrand Russell reflects both the underlying reasons for our despair and the hopelessness of it all in his suggested solution: '' . . . only on the firm foundation of unyielding despair, can the soul's habitation henceforth be safely built.''[17]

IS GOD DEAD?

The various materialist philosophies (evolutionism, humanism, communism) offer us nothing but that which we cannot accept . . . that we are absolutely meaningless. If the very best in life is ultimately meaningless (love, beauty, joy, sharing, intimacy), at least the worst in life is preventable by suicide, *so some say*. Such reasoning has only one origin. When man kills God, he must kill himself, as well. Without God, man is lost. As Sartre noted, without an infinite reference point, it is impossible for man to have any meaning. Those who kill God soon feel the consequences. Theodore Rozak in his *Where the Wasteland Ends* refers to the result of the cultural death of God: '' . . . The void beyond. And only to glimpse that nothingness wherein all things human become 'nothing but' . . . 'nothing but' . . . 'nothing but' . . . is to taste the cosmic absurdity, the annihilating despair.''[18] Nietzsche tells us that the inhumane aspects of man ''are perhaps the fertile soil out of which alone all humanity . . . can grow,''[19] and then proceeds to shatter us entirely by having the Madman state:

> Whither is God? I shall tell you. We *have killed him*—you and I. All of us are his murderers. But how have we done this? How were we able to drink up the sea? Who gave us the sponge to wipe away the entire horizon? What did we do when we unchained this earth from its sun? Whither is it moving now? Away from all suns? Are we not plunging continually? Backward, sideward, forward, in all directions? Is there any

up or down left? Are we not straying through an infinite nothing? Do we not feel the breath of empty space? Has it not become colder? Is not night and more night coming on all the while? . . . What was holiest and most powerful of all that the world has yet owned has bled to death under our knives. Who will wipe this blood off us?[20]

Walter Kaufman comments that, "Nietzsche prophetically envisages himself as a madman: to have lost God means madness; and when mankind will discover that it has lost God, universal madness will break out."[21]

When man is separate from God, he is dead—even while he lives. Jesus noted this by referring to the dead who buried their own dead (Matthew 8:22). There is a great deal of interest today in the topic of death, sparked by the "clinical death research" of Drs. Raymond Moody and Elizabeth Kubler-Ross. This involves people who were declared clinically dead but "came back" with stories of their spirit living on in another dimension. This phenomena may indicate both the existence of the human spirit and its survival of death, although there may also be a Faustian bargain in operation. Interested readers may pursue this idea further in John Weldon's *Is There Life After Death?* (Harvest House, 1977). Regardless, we all obviously live and we all shall obviously die. But what we want is to know the meaning of life and death. Why should we die at all? Is the next life worth living if it is but an endless repetition of life on earth?

IS THERE NOTHING MORE?

Religion has traditionally answered the questions with which philosophy and science are incapable of dealing. The problem is that there are so many conflicting religions. Which are really true? Do they all lead to God? Are they all essentially the same? Are they all glorified human philosophy, or are any revealed religion—true communications from God Himself? Is any one in particular entirely unique from the others? In many of the world's major religions (Hinduism, Buddhism, etc.), when you die, the individual known as *you,* is gone forever and ever. (In this respect they share the viewpoint of the materialist philosophies—evolutionism, communism, humanism, etc.) This is true even of reincarnation, for although the soul supposedly has innumerable incarnations, it is never again the same person and ultimately it advances by cosmic evolution until it is absorbed into Brahman, Nirvana, or some other form of, essentially, nothingness. The individual is forever obliterated. Again, in this respect, these religions are but variations of materialism and its nihilism. Others teach a supposed eternal existence of the same kind of life that we have now—one involving good and evil— except we live in the spirit world. What many people call "hell on earth" is extended forever into the next life. Again, reflecting modern materialist systems, they believe no real God exists.[22] Apart from Christianity, Judaism, and Islam, these two views represent the vast majority of all religious beliefs. It might be interesting to compare the eleven living religions as to whether or not they believe in a supreme personal God.

> Buddhism—No (polytheistic)
> Jainism—No (atheistic)
> Confucianism—No (defined impersonally as "Heaven" or polytheistic)
> Zoroastrianism—No (an eternal dualism of good and evil)
> Shintoism—No (polytheistic)
> Hinduism—No (the impersonal Brahman)
> Taoism—No (the impersonal Tao)
> Sikhism—No (an abstract Being, largely undefined)
> Islam—Yes
> Christianity—Yes
> Judaism—Yes

Hence, nearly every religion either leaves man meaning-

less (with no supreme personal Being) or eventually an-
nihilates him. Only in the (Islamic) Koran and the Bible do
we find both an infinite-personal God and eternal personal
existence in a perfect state, though we could question
whether the overly materialistic and boring Islamic heaven
could be called "perfect"—the term "improved" would
be more appropriate. (Although looking down and seeing
your friends being fed boiling water in hell forever might
be somewhat disconcerting—Sura 37). The Bible is unique
in its assurance that those who have trusted God will live
forever *as who they are* but perfected in *every* sense of the
term—morally, physically, and spiritually. They will live as
perfect creatures in a perfect environment that will be far
from boring, involving eternal love, joy, and challenge
(Philippians 3:20-21; Ephesians 2:4-9; Revelation 21:1-7,
etc.). The biblical view gives man's life, and even his
sufferings, real meaning because the God Who is there has
Himself lived as a man and suffered as a man. In the end,
there will be seen a divine purpose for everything, and even
in what we can't understand today, we are given the promise that, "God causes all things to work together for
good to those who love Him, to those who are called
according to His purpose" (Romans 8:28). The infinite,
personal God who cares created man in His image, actually
became a Man in the Person of Christ (Philippians 2:5-9;
Colossians 2:9), and, unbelievably, died for man to bring
him back into fellowship with Himself. (The idea is entirely
unique in the history of human thought.) This gives man a
significance and dignity he can find in no other religion or
philosophy that has ever existed on earth. Man is not pri-
mordial slime or a "sick fly." He is infinitely loved by
the infinite God Whose perfect character is never compromised or altered in all eternity. Whatever questions
are raised by the existence of evil, the judgment of Christ
shows God can never compromise His holiness. If the
perfect God Who never changes does indeed love each of
us, there is hope—both now and forever. A great many
people would say, "If only it were true, *but how could we
ever know?*"

WHY THE BIBLE?

This has been a book touching on Bible prophecy. But why the Bible—of all the world's scriptures? We obviously cannot go into *all* the reasons why we believe the Bible is the uniquely revealed Word of God, but we can mention some of them and provide references for future study. There exists a great deal of powerful evidence for the truth of the Christian scriptures. Some of the greatest minds in history have believed the Bible to be the literal Word of God—Jesus Christ, Augustine, Thomas Aquinas, Pascal, John Locke, Sir Issac Newton, C. S. Lewis, etc. In virtually every academic profession, brilliant scholars have believed the same. For example A. E. Wilder-Smith has three doctorate degrees in science. Shildes Johnson, also has three recognized doctorate degrees. Benjamin B. Warfield held four doctorates in theology. R. D. Wilson, the Old Testament scholar of Princeton, was at home in 45 languages and dialects and challenged anyone to make an attack against the Old Testament on the basis of evidence he could not investigate personally. Despite decades of investigating the claims of skeptics, he died a firm believer in the Old and New Testaments as the literal Word of God. Most of the founders of modern science were creationists, many of whom believed in the Bible.[23]

Even those non-commital or hostile to Christianity are forced to acknowledge its uniqueness. Thomas H. Huxley, the antagonist of Christianity and originator of the term "agnostic" stated: "The doctrines of . . . original sin, of the innate depravity of man . . . of the primacy of Satan in this world . . . faulty as they are, appear to me to be vastly nearer the truth than the liberal, popular illusions that babies are all born good . . . and other optimistic figments."[24]

Alan Watts, prophet of Western Zen said of Jesus, "Even to the atheists, he is the supremely good man, the exemplar and moral authority with whom no one may disagree."[25] W. E. H. Lecky, the noted 19th century historian, stated that: "The character of Jesus has not only been the highest pattern of virtue, but the strongest incentive to its practice, and has exerted as deep an influence, that it may be truly said, that the simple record of three short years of active life has done more to regenerate and soften mankind, than all the disquisitions of philosophers and than all the exhortations of moralists."[26]

There are a variety of evidences which, taken together, leave us no other option than to trust the Bible implicitly in all that it says. We will examine only five areas. The weight of the evidence is such in each area that it would stand up in a court of law. None of the scriptures of other world religions can make a similar claim. First, the books of the Bible were copied precisely and accurately over the centuries. The Old Testament was transcribed more accurately than any other ancient book; the New Testament has at least 100 times the textual evidence for its accuracy than any other ancient book. If any book is accurate and reliable, the Bible is. Interested readers should consult Dr. F. F. Bruce's *The New Testament Documents: Are They Reliable,* Dr. R. D. Wilson's *A Scientific Investigation of the Old Testament,* and Drs. Geisler and Nix's *A General Introduction to the Bible.* In 1900 years there have been many critics who have attempted to prove it essentially an inaccurate book. Despite massive investigations by brilliant men, no one has succeeded. No deception has *ever* been found in it and if this says anything, it says its writers were impeccably honest. There is no fact of science, archaeology, history, or medicine that is contrary to it. Second, it is the most universal book in the world. Either the entire Bible or portions of it have been translated into over 1,600 languages. Even modern best sellers are only published in 30 languages. Third, it contains a great deal of documented, genuine, and specific predictions of the future which have been 100% accurate. Few, if any, other scriptures contain valid specific prophecy of the type the Bible has, and none can claim to be errorless. Interested readers should consult Dr. A. C. Custance's *Striking Fulfillments of Prophecy*[27] and Josh McDowell's *Evidence That Demands A Verdict.*

Fourth, where allowed to flourish the Bible has had more of a positive effect on mankind than any other book—culturally, morally, and spiritually.[28] Fifth, the resurrection of Christ is one of the best attested facts of history. Brook Foss Wescott, the English scholar at Cambridge, stated: "Indeed, taking all the evidence together, it is not too much to say that there is no historic incident better or more variously supported than the resurrection of Christ."[29] Dr. J. W. Montgomery states, "The evidence for it is tremendous . . . ."[30] John Singleton Copley, recognized as one of the greatest legal minds in British history, stated: "Such evidence for the resurrection has never broken down yet."[31] Such statements could be multiplied a hundred fold. The resurrection itself is the foundation of proof—there is no Christianity without it. It is unique among the world's religions and the evidence of the truthfulness of Jesus' claims and deity. It is proof our sins have been forgiven (Romans 4:25; 6:23). To disregard the Bible as God's word, unbelief has to explain away the Bible's uniqueness, miracles, textual, archaeological, and historical reliability, its immense claims, prophetic, medical, and scientific accuracy;[32] how the writers often corrected erroneous cultural beliefs of their times, its indestructibility, despite great persecution (e.g. the Diocletian edict of 303 A.D.), and its universal appeal. Then there are other factors which, *in their historical setting* make no sense at all unless its message is true. The changed lives of the apostles, the conversion of Saul, the existence of the Christian church and its initial formation by devout Jews, the miraculously changed lives throughout history when one "receives Christ," the existence of the Jew, the person of Christ and His trust in the Bible, and the unique salvation it offers.

How are we to explain the existence of a book, 2000-3,500 years old, with no proven errors in it, referring to scores of controversial subjects without disagreement, speaking with equal authority about the unknown as it does the known (e.g. life after death, the nature of God, etc.), having more of an impact historically than any other book in existence, containing the greatest teachings man has ever known, since which time there has been no improvement, being the most universal book in the world and the only one among all religions offering salvation as a free gift apart from personal merit? How can we explain these and other profound facts when we consider the Bible had some 40 different authors, was written over a time span of 1,500 years, on three continents (Africa, Asia, Europe), in three languages (Hebrew, Aramaic, Greek) by every class of men from fishermen and peasants to philosophers, physicians, poets, statesmen, scholars, and kings? We cannot think of any other reasonable explanation than what the Bible itself claims repeatedly—that God inspired the writers to record what He wanted men to know.

THE CONVERSIONS OF SKEPTICS

One of the easiest ways to become converted to Christianity is to try to disprove it. One of the first and most intense skeptics, Saul of Tarsus, was converted by rather direct evidence and became the Apostle Paul (Acts 22). In the mideighteenth century George Lyttelton (a member of Parliament and Commissioner of the Treasury) and Gilbert West were both given a year's time in which to disprove Christianity, one by showing the resurrection untrue and the other by invalidating the conversion of Saul. Both became converts, and their correspondence provides an admirable defense for Christianity. This can be found in the Early American Imprints #8909 (1639-1800) of the American Antiquarian Society (Readex Microprint AC-4-E15). Frank Morrison, an atheist lawyer of the 1930's, set out to write a book disproving the resurrection and was converted before he could write the second chapter. His story appears in his *Who Moved the Stone?* C. S. Lewis, the brilliant Cambridge scholar, was converted from atheism and into the kingdom of God on the basis of the evidence. This story appears in *Surprised by Joy.* His book on Christian evidences, *Mere Christianity,* is one of the best available and was responsible for the conversion of Charles Colson *(Born Again).* Josh

McDowell used to think that every Christian had two minds: one was lost, and the other was out looking for it. After being challenged to really investigate the evidence, he did so, recognizing that if he were to be intellectually honest, there was no other choice. The result was his conversion and eventually one of the modern classics for the historical evidence of Christianity, the two volume *Evidence That Demands A Verdict* and *More Than A Carpenter*. Sir William Ramsey, the noted archaeologist and skeptic was converted by trying to disprove the authenticity of the writings of Luke through personal archaeological investigation. His findings converted him. Then he believed that "Luke's history is unsurpassed in respect of its trustworthiness," and that "Luke is a historian of the first rank . . . . In short, this author should be placed along with the very greatest of historians."[33] Luke, himself a physician trained in precision, states he "examined everything carefully" so as to write "the exact truth" about what had happened. He refers to Christ presenting Himself alive after his death "by many convincing [decisive] proofs" (Luke 1; Acts 1). We could go on and on citing the testimony of conversions of skeptics, but the point is made. The evidence is sufficient to stand up against the most rigorous of honest investigations. The interested reader could pursue this in a number of excellent, challenging volumes: J. N. D. Anderson's *Christianity and Comparative Religion,* Francis Schaeffer's *He Is There and He Is Not Silent,* John W. Montgomery's *Christianity For The Tough-Minded,* Henry M. Morris' *Many Infallible Proofs,* etc.

Christianity is not just intellectual, it is intensely practical in daily living—providing hope, assurance, meaning to life, and intimate relationship with a God Who personally loves you infinitely. Regardless of your altering circumstance and changing emotions, this God Who comes into your life to live with you and guide you says, "I will never leave you or forsake you," and that *nothing* shall ever separate you from His love (Hebrews 13:5; Romans 8:28-38). There is the promise of substantial healing now in mind and body and the guarantee of an eternal life in glory after death (I John 5:13).

THE MORAL ISSUE

The question of morality is a most important one. The level of morality in any society is proportional to its quality of life. It affects each of us personally. The lack of morality in any institution corrupts it—be it government or marriage. Who today is not concerned about crime in our society? Obviously, if we extend this into the eternal state, it is of utmost concern to know if there is a holy and just God ruling the universe, or an evil or arbitrary one. If we examine all the living world religions, we can only find one truly moral God. As Dr. Hume states in his assessment of the eleven living religions, "Christianity is unique as regards the moral character of God . . . . [None] present a deity who in his own character is self-sacrificingly seeking the redemption of the world, and who in human history has been represented by a person of that same moral character. Christianity's doctrine of monotheism has the highest possible moral content—a holy, loving, heavenly Father, Who actively seeks the welfare, trust, obedience, cooperation, love, and worship of all mankind."[34] By studying other gods we come to appreciate the biblical God more fully. The lower Hindu and Buddhist gods are morally imperfect and often outrightly evil. They are more demons than gods. The highest Hindu "God," the impersonal Brahman is *beyond* good and evil, so that they are both one to "It." "It" remains ever unconcerned with the "creation" since it is its *maya* (illusion) and exists only for its *lila* (sport or play). Nothing except Brahman really exists, and there is no significance to history, human existence, or morality. Indra, one of Brahman's incarnations, seems even to boast of his evil nature and unconcern with human life. "The man who knows me as I [truly] am loses nothing whatever he does. Even if he kills his mother or father, even if he steals or procures an abortion; for whatever evil he does, he does not blanch if he knows me as I am."[35] To know the Eastern gods as they truly are is to know they are evil beings. In the Bhagavad Gita, Krishna tells the struggling warrior Arjuna that he has to "attain a state of consciousness which will justify any action of his and will allow him even to kill in love, in support of the purpose of evolution."[36] According to this "God", "even if a devotee commits the most abominable actions he is to be considered saintly."[37] Here we have the philosophy of the Manson cult. Just how close the two really are has been documented in "The Manson Factor" in John Weldon's *The Transcendental Explosion*. In essence, Eastern religions are both inherently evil and antisocial. For example, guru Bubba Free John in his *Garbage and the Goddess* states:

> Motherhood is garbage. Children are garbage. It is all garbage . . . . It is not that all human beings are literally garbage and should be sent to the gas chamber, but your whole participation in existence, the whole drama of existence that you ordinarily cognize and demonstrate from hour to hour, is garbage.[38]

In teaching a radical social anarchy to be free of "the illusion," his community of disciples have destroyed themselves in the name of "spirituality." *Apart from the biblical God, there is no God of absolute goodness.* Allah, the Islamic God does not forgive men on the basis of justice, but simply on the basis of his arbitrary will. As we have seen, Islam is the only other religion that could be said to have a true God in the sense of God being both infinite and personal. Anything less simply is not God. It is important to note here that a culture's religious belief greatly influences its level of prosperity and quality of life. The rat worship, bondage to multitudinous gods of evil, disease, and murder, eating of cow dung and urine (as well as dead bodies) that occur in India result directly from the Hindu religion.[39] The suffering is unimaginable; the poverty and the millions of lives lived in abject misery are tragic. In a nation of starving people, the cows and rats are well fed. Rats alone, incidentally, eat enough food to feed 20,000,000 people a year. In the West, we live far better largely because our nations were founded upon the Christian world view—of a God Who cares, of man having significance, of a distinction between good and evil, etc. The cost of a culture abandoning the true God is always deep and severe, and unless our country turns back to God, we will suffer a similar fate.

In Islam, because of the teachings in the Koran, there is a fatalism that pervades its adherents and influences the culture, and the Islamic God cannot be held to be morally perfect. G. Margoliouth says in the introduction to J. M. Rodwell's translation, "The shortcomings of the moral teaching contained in the Koran are striking enough . . . . "[40] Hume states, "Moral culpability in the character of Allah is repeatedly denied in the Koran (2:24; 4:44; 28:14). But more frequently affirmed is the absolute arbitrariness of Allah . . . . Equally explicit are the statements that Allah misleads certain people [to send them to hell] (13:33; 14:32; 40:35, 36, 74; 61:5)."[41] Allah would never stoop so low as to become a man, let alone die for man—the very idea is blasphemous to a Muslim. This again points out the uniqueness of the Christian God. He is humble and caring. When Jesus washed the disciples feet, wept over Jerusalem, held children in his arms, and forgave his murderers, it was God Himself doing these things. A comparison of the Bible and the Koran bears out the contrasts between the two Gods. In the Koran, which is held to be divinely inspired, as is the Bible, women are inherently inferior and are to be beaten if they are disobedient (Sura 4, "women"). In the Bible, women are not inherently inferior, and wife beating is forbidden. Husbands are to love their wives just as Christ loved the Church and died for it (Ephesians 5:25-30), and women are to respect their husbands. The Koran teaches you will be saved if you believe in Allah and His prophet, if you do all that Allah requires of you (various religious duties, etc.), and if, on the judgment day, your good deeds out-weigh your bad deeds . . . and even then only if Allah so wills it. No Muslim can know they are saved until they die.[42] The Bible teaches that a person is saved simply by faith, *plus nothing.* No good works, no pilgrimages, no church attendance, just believing that Christ died for you personally. And once we do truly believe, God changes us and makes us better persons by slowly conforming us to the image of Christ. We can have assurance that we will spend eternity with God when we die. "These things I have written you who believe in the name of the Son of God in order that you may *know* you have eternal life" (I John 5:13). The Koran, as well as the scriptures of all other religions, contain numerous errors and moral abberations which are difficult to harmonize with benevolent all-knowing God; e.g., the Koran teaches that Jesus didn't die on the cross. If we know one thing about Jesus, we know He died on the cross.[43] In Sura 4, the Koran teaches us to "Seek out your enemies relentlessly . . . . You shall not plead for traitors." If converts fall away and become hypocrites, they are to be seized "and put to death wherever you find them." "The unbelievers are your sworn enemies." In contrast, Jesus said, "You have heard that it was said 'You shall love your neighbor and hate your enemy' but I say to you, love your enemies and pray for those who persecute you, in order that you may be sons of your Father Who is in heaven" (Matthew 5:44-45). The Bible says unbelievers are to be loved, cared for, and prayed for (Romans 10:1-4; Matthew 5:44-48), because God loves both the sinful and unbelievers. Allah does not love the sinful and can abandon even believers if he so desires (Sura 3, 4). The orthodox Muslim cannot say "God is love." Neither can the Hindu, whose god (Brahman) is impersonal and devoid of any attributes, or the Buddhist who denies an absolute being. Only the Christian can say, "God is love" (I John 4:16), because God has proven his love. God actually died for the sinful and will never leave or forsake those who place trust in Him (John 3:16; Romans 5:6-11; 8:38-9; Ephesians 2:1-9; Hebrews 13:5). It is clear that all religions are not alike as it is clear that common sense dictates the best God to follow is the biblical one.

THE INNATE NEED FOR GOD

There are no other answers. As Dr. Schaeffer points out so well in his *He Is There and He Is Not Silent,* it's not just that Christianity is the best answer, it's that it is the *only* answer. Every other religion or philosophy leads down a dead end road to despair. Only Christianity offers hope. It alone has the answers to the problem of metaphysics (existence), morals, and epistemology (how we know what is true). No other system has the answers to the deep questions men have asked. Christianity can be pressed to its logical conclusion and it will be true to what is there.

Interested readers should pursue Dr. Schaeffer's fascinating book, however the point we wish to emphasize is that you can search the world over and you will find nothing like it—only Christianity has an infinitely loving and holy God, provides the guarantee of salvation in this life, offers this salvation in an instantaneous free gift conditioned only upon receiving it, and has God come and dwell within you forever (John 14:23).

In this book we have examined the desperate condition of our world—ecologically, militarily, and economically. We have seen the kind of hope the world offers, and it has not been easy to take. Statements like the following by Chou-En-Lai are far too common among those who control over ⅓ of the world. "The revolutionary people do not at all believe in a so-called 'lasting peace' or a 'generation of peace'. So long as imperialism exists, revolution and war are inevitable."[44] So much for the communist view of détente. In our final chapter, we have examined despair of modern man and turned of necessity to a higher reality in search of hope and truth. We examined the main world religions, but again found only despair, with one exception. We must understand that as twisted as many religions are, they all reflect an innate need for God. This is how He created us—in His image, with the need to trust in Him. We are not gods—we are simple finite creatures in need of their Creator. We need to go back Home.

Despite the modern disdain for God in academic and scientific circles, we can see the truth if we will just open our eyes a little. The dean of existentialism, Jean Paul Sartre, stated: "God is silent and that I cannot deny; everything in myself calls for God and that I cannot forget."[45] An amazing statement coming from whom it does? Not really! We all cry out for God—in ways we don't even recognize. God is not the one Who is silent. He has spoken clearly in the Bible. We are the ones who have rejected Him. The silence is on our part. We cry out "God where are You?" but we don't listen to what He has said. He has sent His Son, but we will not respond to Him. What we need to do is stop fighting and give in. The purpose of all life is to know this God personally.

Many other things could be said about why the biblical God is the only true God, but enough has been said already. It is logical that there is only one true God, and if you desire a God of love, justice, and compassion, there is only one available. In our modern world of ecumenism and religious syncretism, such a statement is profound, but it is impeccably logical—and true.

THE PERSONAL CHALLENGE

God offers anyone all that they have ever desired in life—real love, peace, joy, and challenge. Living with God isn't always easy, but He always sees us through the difficult moments. And living *with* God is far easier than living *without* Him. God truly does love man and wants each one to come to know Him and discover the purpose for their existence.

> For God so loved the world, that He gave His only begotten Son that whoever believes in Him should not perish but have everlasting life (John 3:16).

> . . . in order that in the ages to come He might

> show the surpassing riches of His grace in kindness toward us in Christ Jesus (Ephesians 2:7).

Shortly after His resurrection, Jesus ascended into heaven, but before he left, He promised to return for His followers. In this book, we have pointed out many problems in the world, but these have been *predicted* to occur just prior to the Second Coming of Christ. The world has lost hope of solving all its problems, but that does not mean there is no hope. The true hope of the world is the personal return of Jesus Christ. As He promised, the Lord will come again and take care of the mess that man has made of his world. Jesus told His disciples, "For the Son of Man is going to come in the glory of His Father with His angels, and will then recompense every man according to His deeds" (Matthew 16:27). God doesn't like the condition of the world any better than you or we. In fact, He is outraged by it and will judge it for its evil. When the world turns so far from God as to even worship Satan as God (in the person of the antichrist, the coming world dictator), this will mark the beginning of God's judgments. During this time, the world will feel the full wrath of God for all its evil. At the end of this period, Christ will return from heaven in glory and remove all wickedness from the earth.

> The Lord Jesus shall be revealed from heaven with His mighty angels in flaming fire dealing out retribution to those who do not know God and to those who do not obey the gospel of our Lord Jesus (II Thessalonians 1:7-8).

He will then begin His peaceful reign. Finally, all the insoluble problems with which man has wrestled for the ages will be removed. There will be no more starvation, wars, pollution, or wasted billions on armaments. The world shall be a virtual Garden of Eden, and men shall live in harmony. It is comforting to realize that everything the Bible has said will come to pass has done so; therefore, the return of Christ is likewise assured. Today, although the second coming is viewed as a religious myth (even this was predicted—II Peter 3:3-4), the proof that it will occur is in the proven prophetic record of the Bible. The Word of God is replete with promises about the return of Christ.

> . . . looking for that blessed hope and the glorious appearing of our great God and Savior Jesus Christ (Titus 2:13).

> Behold, He is coming with the clouds and every eye will see Him, even those who pierced Him, and all the tribes of the earth will mourn over Him. Even so. Amen. I am the Alpha and Omega says the Lord God, who is and who was and who is to come, the Almighty (Revelation 1:7-8).

Jesus said, "For just as the lightning comes from the east and flashes even to the west, so shall the coming of the Son of Man be" (Matthew 24:27). However, as fantastic as the return and rule of Christ will be, it is only the beginning. For all eternity, those who have trusted Christ will live in a universe of perfection that knows no bounds or end to holiness, love, joy, and peace. The God "who is able to do exceedingly abundantly beyond all that we ask or think" (Ephesians 3:20) has prepared an eternity for us beyond our wildest imaginations. We shall soon inherit it, and only then shall we realize the full meaning of the promise:

> Things which eye has not seen and ear has not heard and which have not entered into the heart of man, all that God has prepared for those who love him (I Corinthians 2:9).

The condition of the world doesn't reflect God's character—the Bible does that. The condition of the world reflects Satan's character and the fallen character of man.

Satan is called "the god of this world" (II Corinthians 4:4), and he is working to build his kingdom. However, "God is light, and in Him there is no darkness at all" (I John 1:5).

Since God could never compromise His holiness, He had to devise a way to retain His righteousness and yet to forgive man for his sins. He judged Christ in our place, so that simply by believing in Him, we are forgiven. God is an infinitely loving (although infinitely holy) Being Who asks only one thing of men and women—simply that they be honest with themselves in recognizing that they stand before Him in need of forgiveness. We have broken His laws and need to set things straight, so to speak, with our God.

He is so holy He will not (He cannot) accept into His presence anything less than perfect. If we do not receive His forgiveness in this life we must live forever separated from Him in the next life. This, too, is only logical. People do not evolve to somewhere "out there," as many religions would teach. All who have not been forgiven, are in a place of punishment that will never end. (In the eternal state, unless punishment is everlasting, it is without meaning. Since God's love also demands He be absolutely just, His justice can never be compromised, as it would have to be, if He were to punish us for a *time,* and then bring us into heaven *forever.)* As the Bible states, we can, by our pride and rebellion "reject God's purpose for us" (Luke 7:30). God has done everything He could do. It's now up to each of us. There is one requirement. We must each make the decision, before God, to turn to Christ—to trust Him for forgiveness of sins. When Jesus was asked by concerned people what work they must perform for God, he replied, "This is the work of God, that you believe in Him Whom He has sent." (John 6:29). This belief is not a cultural "acceptance" of Christ—a tag you wear just because you were raised in a "Christian" culture. It is a personal trust of one's self to Christ, receiving Him into our lives.

Each person has the choice. We can continue to be

nominal Christians with emptiness deep inside. We can continue to be "nonreligious," i.e. to live with a material-istic outlook, living only for ourselves, so aware of the pain and meaningless of existence we have to fill our lives with innumerable distractions and not allow ourselves to really *think* about "Who am I?" "Why am I here?" "Where am I headed?" We can turn to Eastern religions or the despair of modern philosophy or humanism, or to the continual "revolutionary wars" of communism. We can turn to the occult, but 9 out of 10 who do so suffer serious psychopathology and spiritual disorders as a re-sult,[46] to say nothing of the hereditary effects upon the children, which ruin their lives as well.[47] Then there is always the arbitrary God of Islam, who gives us no guarantee of salvation and can turn against us if He so chooses. Or we can turn to a God of both infinite love and justice, Who loved us so much He actually died for us and bore the punishment due us in His own Person (II Corinthians 5:21; Acts 20:28) . . . He Who says, "I came that they might have life and have it abundantly that My joy might be in them, and their joy might be made full" (John 10:10; 15:11) . . . the One Who uncon-ditionally guarantees our salvation if we will but turn to Him (Hebrews 6:17-20).

The choice we have is clear. We can choose between many different gods, all of whom can only be described as inherently evil, indifferent, unloving, or impersonal, or to one unique God Who is so different that in space-time history, He demonstrated His love and concern:

> For God so loved the world that He gave His only begotten Son that whoever believes in Him
> · should not perish, but have everlasting life (John 3:16).

Coming events cast their shadows. We who write this book look for Christ's return as a personal vital hope. What about you? It can be the hope of each of us, you included, if in sincerity you will pray this prayer:

Lord Jesus Christ, I'm a sinner in need of salvation. You died for sinners—and that includes me. I ask you to come into my life, to be my Savior. Give me the desire and the strength to live for You a life that is pleasing to you, from this day onward. Amen.

Christ offers life, purpose, hope. You need not fear the many impending crises, for the ultimate reality is in the realm of the spiritual, and that is where your eternal home will be. So it is that we commend to you Jesus Christ Who said of Himself:

I am the way, the Truth, and the life. No man comes to the Father but by Me (John 14:6).

Footnotes: Chapter 18

1. *The Death of Adam, Evolution and Its Impact on Western Thought,* (Iowa State University Press, 1959), p. 338.
2. *Life Against Death,* (London: Sphere books, 1968), p. 267. From Os Guinness, *The Dust of Death,* (Inter-Varsity, 1973), p. 13.
3. *The New Priesthood,* (New York: Harper and Row, 1961), p. 29. From Alvin Toffler, *Future Shock,* (Bantam, 1974), p. 431.
4. Interview, *And It Is Divine,* May, 1973, p. 58.
5. *Back To Freedom and Dignity,* (Downers Grove: Inter-Varsity, 1972) p. 26.
6. *Time,* March 18, 1974, p. 66.
7. Taken from the English Summary, available from E.P.M., Box 5083, Station B., Victoria, B.C., $2.00; p. 1212, 1240.

8. Clark Pinnock, *Set Forth Your Case,* (Chicago: Moody Press, 1971), p. 39.

9. *Being and Nothingness,* (London: Methuen, 1957), p. 566.

10. *The Rebel,* Trans. A. Bower, (Harmondsworth: Penguin, 1962), p. 16. From Guinness, *op. cit.,* p. 37.

11. *The Politics of Ecstacy,* (New York: World Publishing Co., 1968), p. 321.

12. *Los Angeles Times,* Calendar section, August 5, 1973, p. 54.

13. Clark Pinnock, *Live Now Brother,* (Chicago: Moody Press, 1972), p. 18.

14. Fyodor Dostoyevsky, "Notes From the Underground" (selections); Eric and Mary Josephson (Eds.), *Man Alone: Alienation in Modern Society,* (New York: Dell, 1964), p. 368-369.

15. Interview, *Los Angeles Times,* June 24, 1973, part 7, p. 1.

16. *Collegiate Challenge,* Vol. 8, No. 2, p. 25; Campus Crusade for Christ, Arrowhead Springs, San Bernardino, CA.

17. *Why I Am Not A Christian and Other Essays,* (New York: Simon & Schuster, 1957), p. 107.

18. (New York: Anchor Books, 1973), p. 172.

19. Walter Kaufman, *Nietzsche,* (New York: Vintage, 1968), p. 193; citing Homers Contest (1872) II, 369.

20. *Ibid.,* p. 97, citing *The Gay Science,* (1882), p. 125.

21. *Ibid.*

22. See the comparison of the 11 major religions in Robert Humes, *The World's Living Religions,* (New York: Charles Schribners Sons, 1959), ch. 13.

23. R. L. Wysong, *The Creation-Evolution Controversy,* (East Lansing, MI: Inquiry Press, Box 1766, 48823), 1976, p. 417-8.

24. David Lack, *Evolutionary Theory and Christian Belief,* (London: Methuen, 1957), p. 108.

25. Robert Sohl and Audrey Carr (Eds.), *The Gospel According to Zen,* (New York: Mentor, 1970), p. 16.

26. *History of European Morals from Augustine to Char-*

lemagne, 2nd. edition, (London: Longmans, Green, 1869), Vol. II, p. 88. From J. W. Montgomery, *History and Christianity,* (Downers Grove: Inter-Varsity), 1969, p. 62.

27. Currently republished in the 10 volume Doorway Paper Series from Zondervan Publishers.

28. e.g. J. Edwin Orr, *The Light of the Nations;* Tim LaHaye, *The Bible's Influence on American History,* (San Diego: Master Books, 1977); Donald McGavran, "Support the Church for the Good of Society", *Christianity Today,* April 7, 1978, p. 34, 39.

29. *The Gospel of the Resurrection,* (1879), 4th. ed., p. 4-6.

30. *History and Christianity, op. cit.,* p. 76.

31. Wilbur Smith, *Therefore Stand,* (Grand Rapids: Baker Book House, 1972), p. 425, 584.

32. cf. S. I. McMillen, M.D., *None of These Diseases,* (medical), (Old Tappan, NJ: Revelle, 1970); Clifford Wilson's, *That Incredible Book the Bible,* (archaeology), (Melbourne: Word of Truth, 1973). On Science see material from the Institute for Creation Research, 2716 Madison Avenue, San Diego, CA 92116.

33. F. F. Bruce, *The New Testament Documents,* (Downers Grove, IL: Inter-Varsity, 1965), p. 90-91.

34. Robert Hume, *The World's Living Religions,* (New York: Charles Schribners Sons, 1959), p. 271.

35. Kaushitaki Upanishad 3:1-2.

36. Maharishi Mahesh Yogi, *On the Bhagavad Gita,* a commentary on vs. 1-6, (New York: Penguin, 1974), p. 76.

37. A.C.B. Prabhupada, *Back to Godhead,* magazine #55, p. 25, ISCKON International, (Hare Krishna), quoting the Bhagavad Gita 9:30.

38. (Lower Lake, CA: The Dawn Horse Press, 1974), p. 120.

39. John Weldon, *The Transcendental Explosion,* (Irvine: Harvest House, 1976), ch. 6.

40. (New York: Dutton, Everyman's Library, 1977), p. viii.

41. Hume, *op. cit.,* p. 233.

42. William Miller, *A Christian's Response to Islam,* (Nutley, NJ: Presbyterian and Reformed, 1977), p. 81-83.

43. e.g. cf., Gleason Archer's, *A Survey of Old Testament Introduction,* (Chicago: Moody Press, 1974), Appendix 2, Sura 3, 4, 5; and Rodwell, *op. cit.,* p. 344, note 1, (Sura 2:61).

44. *Time,* April 15, 1974, p. 50.

45. Clark H. Pinnock, "Cultural Apologetics: an Evangelical Standpoint", *Bibliotheca Sacra,* January-March, 1970, p. 61; citing, Charles L. Glicksberg, *Literature and Religion,* p. 221.

46. Kurt Koch, *Occult Bondage and Deliverance,* (Grand Rapids: Kregel, 1969), p. 30.

47. Kurt Koch, *Christian Counseling and Occultism,* (Grand Rapids: Kregel, 1972), pp. 184-187.

Appendix

BUT UNTIL THEN . . .

No matter how bleak the immediate future appears, each person is still responsible for their own actions. Pessimism cannot be made an excuse for irresponsibility. In the 19th chapter of Luke, Christ uses a parable to correct the disciples' mistaken impression that He was going to set up his earthly kingdom immediately. He speaks of a ruler going away and entrusting his servants with the responsibility of diligently being about His business while He was gone. He told them to "occupy till I come [again]." Then when He returned, He called them all in and held them accountable for their actions in His absence.

Even as Christians, we will be held accountable for being good stewards over those things with which the Lord has entrusted us (government, environment, economics, etc.), and let us not forget that human action can change the course of history. Jonah preached that, because of its evil, Nineveh would be overthrown in 40 days by the hand of God. The King and the people heard of the coming judgment and the King issued a decree stating: "Let men call on God earnestly that each may turn from his wicked way and from the violence which is in his hands. Who knows, God may turn and relent, and withdraw His burning anger so that we shall not perish?'' The result is well known: ''When God saw their deeds, that they turned from their wicked way, then God relented.concerning the calamity which He had declared He would bring upon them. And He did not do it'' (Jonah 3). Even Jesus used the lesson of Jonah in a way that is particularly applicable to our own time, with the many forms of wickedness that pervade our society—fornication, adultery, homosexuality, crime, drugs, hedonism, rebellion, occult supernaturalism, etc.:

> An evil and adulterous generation craves for a sign (attesting miracles), and yet no sign shall be given to it but the sign of Jonah the Prophet . . . . The men of Nineveh shall stand up with this generation at the judgment and shall condemn it because they repented (turned to God) at the preaching of Jonah, and behold something greater than Jonah is here (Matthew 12:39-41).

In response to Moses' prayer, the Lord ''repented'' of his intention to destroy the Israelites (because of their worship of the golden calf after He had delivered them out of Egypt). The Bible also tells us that ''the fervent prayer of a *righteous* man availeth much.'' That's what the people of Nineveh did—turned from their wicked ways and fervently (earnestly) called on God.

This, then, is the most important thing we can do for our society—turn to God and Christ and be changed from within. You cannot change yourself, but God can change you into an entirely new person: ''Therefore if any man is in Christ, he is a new creature; the old things passed away; behold, new things have come. Now all these things are from God, Who reconciled us to Himself through Christ . . . . We beg you on behalf of Christ, be reconciled to God'' (II Corinthians 5:17-21). For us to continue as we are will guarantee God's judgment, both as a nation and personally. Whatever the future holds, if we have come to know God, we need not ''give up in despair'' because in trusting our lives to Him we find that: (1) He is trust-worthy; (2) He will work all things together for our good (Romans 8:28); and (3) He desires that we live godly, responsible lives. We can accept reality and also be optimistic, as well as responsible citizens concerned with our society. This is implied in "always seeking after that which is good for one another and for all men" and "loving our neighbor as ourself" (I Thessalonians 5:15; Matthew 19:19). What specifically can we do? First, as previously pointed out, become a Christian. Without this, all the rest is useless. Jesus said, "What will it profit a man to gain the whole world and lose his own soul" (Matthew 16:26). You will find you have new joy, new power, and a desire to love God and man that was never present before. Once you experience the new life in Christ, you'll wish you hadn't waited so long. There is a contentment that comes upon finally knowing truth and having peace with God, and this contentment spills over into all areas of life. It makes us free to live better lives. We no longer have to look out for "number one," abuse drugs and alcohol, manipulate others, etc. Many of the underlying causes for our antihuman behavior—restlessness, fear, need for acceptance, loneliness, anxiety, depression, self-hate, guilt, etc.—are all of a sudden substantially removed in the love of God, and we become much freer to really live life. Those who have a secure place in eternity find it very much easier to put others first.

Second, evangelize—help others turn back to God. A fully changed life committed to principles of biblical morality will do more to help society than anything else. Support evangelistic endeavors with your work and finances.

Third, and this is also important, avoid supporting injurious social trends (occultism, eastern religions, easy abortions, drugs, homosexual activism, pornography, etc.). Many of us, in some way, support one or more of these areas, either directly or indirectly, by not speaking of the consequences when we have the opportunity. How many of us totally ignore God's will in our lives? How many of us play with ouija boards, tarot cards, astrology, or other dangerous practices,[1] or support the local guru? How many of us subscribe to Playboy or go to X and R rated movies which concentrate on degrading women into sex objects and promote violence and dehumanization? How many of us are fornicators or adulterers, helping to destroy the sanctity of marriage and the family, one of the foundations of social order? Pre-Nazi Germany was a culture similar to ours in many ways, with more eastern gurus per capita than we have, interest in the occult, loose moral standards, economic disruption, etc. It was ripe for Hitler.[2]

How many of us spend time at home with our families reading the Bible, or other good literature, together, instead of four hours before the tube?

The 23 inch screen is my shepherd. I shall not want.
  It makes me to lie down in Bonanza country.
It leads me beside idleness.
  It hardens my soul.
It guides me in the paths of "The following program
    is brought to you in living color" . . . for the
    sponsor's sake.
  Yea, though I walk through the hallway for a snack
    at commercial time, I will fear no evil: for the
    sponsor's voice it goes with me.
The channel selector and fine tuning they comfort me.
  It dost prepare a banquet of distraction before me,
    in the presence of my family.
It anoints my head with commercials;
  My cup runneth over with each new season.
Surely the sponsors' and announcers' voices will
    follow me all the days of my life
  And I will dwell in front of the 23 inch screen
    forever.[3]

Our national penchant for occult involvement is serious enough. Most people do not realize that even seemingly innocent occult activities are subtle traps and represent contact with powers alien to God. The severe personal, spiritual, and cultural consequences of occult involvement (and all eastern religions are occult systems) are well documented.[4] Do we love our children enough to discipline them consistently so they know someone cares? Do our daily choices foster intimacy and growth in our family—or estrangement?

Fourth, as a nation we are too wasteful of our resources, especially energy. Europeans have a comparable standard of living on half the per capita energy consumption. Another liability is that we are too concerned with materialism. The suicide rate reflects this—it is higher in rich countries than poor countries. We need to live more frugally, more ecologically, and bring back the virtues of old time morality and hard work. We must reduce our dependence on foreign oil, which is now at the danger level. If the OPEC nations were Marxist, we would probably either have lost our freedoms by now, or started World War III.

Fifth, we should pray—for individuals, for our nation (and its leaders), and for the world. Remember, God's Word promises that the fervent prayer of the righteous avails much.

Finally, we must prepare for the future. In our world a great deal of knowledge—with no wisdom—is dangerous. We should wisely prepare for future difficulties, as Joseph prepared for famine in the time of plenty during the reign of the Egyptian Pharaohs (Genesis 41). There are several helpful books on this.[5] There is also much wisdom offered in the book of Proverbs.

As Dr. Schaeffer states, "The choices we make in the next decade will mold irrevocably the direction of our culture and the lives of our children." Most of our problems result from our rebellion against our Creator. If we haven't yet come to know Him, the time has come to make a choice.

Footnotes: Appendix

1. See Ed. Gruss, *The Ouija Board: Doorway to the Occult;* Koch, *Between Christ and Satan; The Devil's Alphabet.*
2. John De Graaf, "The Wandervogel", *New Age Journal,* March, 1978, p. 44; Joe Hunt, "Blissing out in Valhalla", *New Age Journal,* #4.
3. Adapted and revised from an article by David Kirby in *For Real,* Vol. 2, no. 2.
4. Gary North, (Ed.), "Magic, Envy, and Economic Underdevelopment", *Journal of Christian Reconstruction,* Vol. 1, no. 2, Symposium on Satanism, Chalcedon Publishers, Box 158, Vallecito, CA 95251; Gary North, *None Dare Call It Witchcraft,* (New Rochelle, NY: Arlington House, 1976), chapter 8 and pp. 76, 87, 98, 157-8, 169-75, 195-6, 206, 211; Kurt Koch, *Occult Bondage and Deliverance,* et al; John Weldon, *The Hazards of Occultism,* unpublished manuscript.
5. Paul Ehrlich's, *How to Be a Survivor,* and *The End of Affluence.* Although we cannot support all his suggestions, many are helpful.

Other Books of Interest

Available From
MASTER BOOKS
A Division of CLP
P. O. Box 15666
San Diego, California 92115

CLOSE ENCOUNTERS: A *Better* Explanation

Clifford Wilson and John Weldon

Are UFO's really of extraterrestrial origin? Are they Biblical? Is the movie "Close Encounters" fact or science fiction? Are aliens trying to bring us messages from other galaxies? Have they really abducted earth people? Read an alternate point of view on the subject of UFO's and their occupants. Tells about actually documented "encounters." **No. 034, Paper $2.95**

War of the Chariots

Clifford Wilson

Resulting from a debate with Erich von Däniken, this book refutes von Däniken's latest absurd accusations that Jesus was an astronaut from outer space, as well as many other wild notions. Includes a detailed report on the debate, as well as questions from the floor. **No. 183, Paper $2.95**

Crash Go The Chariots

Clifford Wilson

Newly revised and enlarged, the original book of this title was the near million bestselling answer to von Däniken's theories concerning unexplained happenings and ruins. These revealing answers to mysterious and haunting questions will arouse your curiosity and at the same time provide sensible answers to von Däniken and his often absurd claims. **No. 035, Paper $1.95**

Monkeys Will Never Talk . . . *Or Will They?*

Clifford Wilson, Ph.D.

Is speech a God-given ability . . . or something that evolved by accident? Dr. Wilson tells about the futile efforts to develop speech—or even logical communication—in various species of the animal kingdom. Although best known for his archaeological studies and his books refuting "gods from outer space" theory, Dr. Wilson's primary field is that of psycholinguistics, and he deals with this subject with great expertise.

No. 104, Paper $3.95

East Meets West in THE OCCULT EXPLOSION

Clifford Wilson

Pagan and semi-religious movements are now sweeping Western culture with unusually successful results in securing converts. Spiritism, witchcraft, and other Satanic cults are on the one hand, and transcendental meditation, yoga, Hare Krishna, and other eastern philosophic movements are springing up on the other hand. This evaluation is very timely and has real help for these very confusing times when Satanic power is being felt more than at any other time in history. **No. 113, Paper $1.95**

Ebla Tablets: SECRETS of a Forgotten City

Clifford Wilson

This book by noted archaeologist, Dr. Clifford Wilson, reveals the secrets of the greatest "find" since the Dead Sea Scrolls. An abundance of clay tablets in a buried city in the Tell Mardikh contain such fascinating information as trade documents referring to the Garden of Eden (Dilmun) as an actual geographic location; and a creation tablet remarkably similar to the Hebrew record—*in writing* more than 2000 years before Christ; discusses the Tower of Babel and much more. **No. 052, Paper $1.95**

The Passover Plot—EXPOSED!

Clifford Wilson

An expert challenge to the confused (but widely accepted) imaginings of the book and movie, *The Passover Plot.* Wilson readily substantiates that Christians have not been deceived by a *hoax,* but that the death and resurrection of Jesus, rather than a *plot,* were part of the greatest *plan* of all ages. **No. 125, Paper $2.25**

DINOSAURS: Those Terrible Lizards

Duane T. Gish, Ph.D.

At last! A book for young people from a creationist perspective, on those intriguing dinosaurs. No one living in the world today has ever seen a real live dinosaur—but did people in earlier times live with dinosaurs? Were dragons of ancient legends really dinosaurs? Does the Bible speak about dinosaurs? The answers are in this book! Written by Dr. Gish, noted scientist who is author of the best seller *Evolution? The Fossils Say NO!,* this book is profusely illustrated in color on beautiful 9" x 11" pages. **No. 046, Cloth $5.95**